THIS BOOK BELONGS TO:

Jemima

Brown

ALL THINGS FRIENDSHIP

A Guide to Celebrating Old Friends, Making New Ones, and Navigating Sticky Social Situations

Copyright © 2024 by Rebel Girls, Inc.

Rebel Girls supports copyright. Copyright fuels creativity, encourages diverse voices, promotes free speech, and creates a vibrant culture. Thank you for buying an authorised edition of this book and for complying with copyright laws by not reproducing, scanning, or distributing any part of it in any form without permission. You are supporting indie creators as well as allowing Rebel Girls to publish books for Rebel Girls wherever they may be.

Good Night Stories for Rebel Girls and Rebel Girls are registered trademarks.
Good Night Stories for Rebel Girls and all other Rebel Girls titles are available for bulk purchase for sale promotions, premiums, fundraising, and educational needs. For details, write to sales@rebelgirls.com.

www.rebelgirls.com

Rebel Girls, Inc.
421 Elm Ave.
Larkspur, CA 94939

Authors: Camila Rivera and Sara Jin Li
Art director: Giulia Flamini
Cover and interior illustrator: Edith Kurosaka
Graphic designer: Kristen Brittain
Editor: Jess Harriton
Special thanks: Amy Pfister, Eliza Kirby, Hannah Bennett, Jes Wolfe, Sarah Parvis

Printed in China, 2023
10 9 8 7 6 5 4 3 2 1
001-340080-March'24
ISBN: 979-8-88964-130-8

CONTENTS

Introduction 8

Chapter 1: What Makes a Good Friend? 12
- Qualities to Look for in a Friend 14
- Finding Your People 17
- Choosing Your Friends Wisely 24
- Quiz: What Are You Looking for in a Friend? 26
- Ask the Experts 28

Chapter 2: How to Make Friends 30
- Know What You're Bringing to the Friendship 32
- Birds of a Feather Flock Together 41
- Getting to Know Each Other 44
- Quiz: Where Will You Meet Your Next Best Friend? 48
- Ask the Experts 50

Chapter 3: Being a Good Friend 52
- There's No Friendship Without Support 54
- How to Communicate Effectively 56
- How to Help a Friend Through a Hard Time 65
- The Ins and Outs of Secret-keeping 68
- Quiz: Respect O-meter 70
- Ask the Experts 72

Chapter 4: Different Types of Friendships .. 74

Finding Love in a Hopeless Place 76
When Worlds Collide 80
A Kaleidoscope of Colours 85
The Ebbs and Flows of Friendships 88
Quiz: What Vibe Do You Bring to Your Friend Group? 92
Ask the Experts 94

Chapter 5: When the Road Gets Rocky 96

Cracking the Clique Code 98
SOS: Asking for Help 101
Friends Don't Hurt Friends 105
How to Apologise 109
Quiz: Are You Standing Up for Yourself? 112
Ask the Experts 114

Chapter 6: Mourning a Friendship 116

Best Friends ~~Forever~~ 117
How to Survive a Friend Break-up 124
The Other Side of the Rainbow 128
Quiz: How Should You Mend Your Hurting Heart? 132
Ask the Experts 134

Chapter 7: Celebrating Friendship......136
The Power of Friendship 138
Being Part of the Rebel Girls Sisterhood 142
In Closing, Remember to 147
Quiz: Friendships Around the World 148
Ask the Experts 150

Resources..............................152

Meet the Authors......................153

Meet the Experts.....................154

More from Rebel Girls................155

About Rebel Girls....................159

For more confidence-boosting content, don't miss the *Growing Up Powerful* podcast, available on the Rebel Girls app or wherever you listen to podcasts.

INTRODUCTION

Hi there, Rebels!

We're Sara Jin Li and Camila Rivera. We're the authors of this book – and guess what? We're best friends in real life! We have been each other's true blue* since we met in a book club four years ago. In that time, we've navigated big life events like career changes, cross-country moves, graduations, and so much more. No matter what happens, we know we have each other's back. Together, we wrote *All Things Friendship* because the only thing more special than writing a book is co-writing it with your best friend.

Camila and Sara

Sara: Wow. I can't believe we've been in each other's lives for only four years, but I feel like I've known you my whole life.

Camila: Soooo true. It felt that way right from the start too. I think you said one word to me and I just replied, "Girl, I know." The rest was history.

*true blue (n): as in, the colour of loyalty, trust, and dedication; a true blue friend is one you can always count on.

Sara: Friendship is funny in that way. Like finding someone who speaks the same language as you in a way that no one else does.

Camila: Exactly. That feeling of being perfectly understood is so empowering. I think that's why writing this book with you was so easy. Our friendship has nurtured me in a way that I want to share with the world.

Sara: I feel the same! I always tell people that you bring so much light into my life, so I was excited for this opportunity to talk about our friendship in-depth. I think we both feel similarly in that the older we get, the more we value the people around us.

Camila: We talk about that all the time. We sound like two old grandmas sitting around, griping, "If only we had known!" [Laughs.] It's wild to think about how different it was for us growing up. I'm proud to see the way girls today are lifting each other up and so honoured to offer whatever I can. We get into everything in this book, from how to make friends to how to be a good friend . . .

Sara: And then there are the messy bits. Like dealing with friendship troubles like rumours and secrets and how to cope when it's time to move on from a friendship. I wish I had this blueprint for friendship when I was growing up. I think it's so healthy and incredible that young women are given the tools to build healthy friendships. It's an honour to be the elder passing along the sacred, ancient text of bestiehood.

Camila: It's a solemn duty! If I want our readers to walk away with anything, it's this: healthy relationships are the colour of our world. They have the power to heal us physically – people with strong ties to others live longer, healthier lives.

Sara: Really? Who said that?

Camila: Harvard! Look it up!

Sara: I totally believe it. Once I started prioritising my friendships, every aspect of my life just got better. I feel stronger, not just physically, but emotionally and mentally as well. I can't wait to grow up and live in a giant house by the beach with all of our closest friends.

Camila: Me too. And you know what? I'm pretty proud of the relationships I have in my life in general, but the way our friends supported us throughout the process of writing this book was so sweet.

Sara: Not to mention a ton of fun. I love any opportunity I get to interview my friends, and I'm excited to share these intimate quotes.

Camila: There's so much about the book that I'm excited for the Rebel Girls to read – like the activities! We simply must pat ourselves on the back. Not to brag, but we made the quizzes in this book extra fun.

Sara: And to think that we'll be telling our future kids about the importance of friendship the way we're doing right now. But OK, we might be getting ahead of ourselves now. I'm just so happy to be here in the present, writing this book with you.

Camila: Same, bestie. There's no one else I'd rather do this with. I say this all the time, but it's a dream come true! And it really is all because of the power of friendship.

On that note, without further ado, we present to you *All Things Friendship* with the sincere hope that you find reading it as enlightening and empowering as we did writing it. Enjoy, Rebels!

Sara
"When I am writing to you, my words will be on a blue background."

Camila
"My thoughts are on the pink pages."

CHAPTER 1
WHAT MAKES A GOOD FRIEND?

Rebels, imagine this: I am 12 years old, and the entirety of my adolescence and young adulthood still sprawls out before me. The world is my oyster, and I can be anything and anyone. I have fantastical ideas about what the future holds. And what I want, above all else, is to be independent. I resent needing others and asking for help. I find it frustrating that I can't have sleepovers with my friends all the time or eat what I want for breakfast (ice-cream, obviously).

Did you know horses are born fully formed? Even as foals, they can run. I wished I was like that. I wanted desperately to prove that I could stand on my own from day one. But time and time again, I was reminded that I needed to learn and grow from the people who loved me before I could take on new things. Humans need one another.

I'm lucky in my life to have seen many of my dreams come true (including becoming the co-author of this book). I've acted, I've travelled, I've checked more things off my bucket list than I ever imagined possible at the age of 27. But I've also had times when I felt very lonely, even in the most beautiful of places.

I realised all the success in the world doesn't mean much without a community of people to share it with.

You're at a time in your life filled with a lot of changes. Maybe your family changes. Maybe your friendships look a little different. Maybe you'll find a new interest that takes you down an unexpected road. Nothing is set in stone, especially at your age. But the one constant that will remain true is that you'll be able to return to the safe house of friendship.

And when you're building your own sanctuary, Rebels, make sure that the company you choose will endure all the stormy nights and sunny days. It's what will remain, so know what makes a good friend and invite them into your life with open arms. That's what we'll go over in this chapter because it makes all the difference in the world.

QUALITIES TO LOOK FOR IN A FRIEND

Friendship is a universal concept, yet the idea of what defines a good friend is not. After all, people have different needs. One girl might decide that a good friend will always tell her the truth, *no matter what*, and another might expect that her friend will bend the truth to make her feel better – like that time she got a terrible haircut and her bestie said it looked both totally fierce and unique.

Self-reflection is important when considering what the idea of a "good friend" means to you. Ask yourself: what is important to me? How do I want myself to echo through the community? It isn't something we necessarily choose, but our friends do become our

WHAT THE REBELS SAY

"Many people will walk in and out of your life, but only true friends will leave footprints in your heart."
—Eleanor Roosevelt

representatives in the world. They can open doors for us, lead us through windows, or burn bridges. It took us a long time to learn, but we're glad we did.

Now it's your turn! What's important to you?

If kindness is your biggest priority, then you'll seek out the sweetest in the bunch. If laughing with your friends is a must, then you'll probably look for others with humour similar to your own. If being open-minded is an important value, then you'll probably wind up spending time with friends who are different from you. Sometimes making a check-list can be a helpful way to figure out what you want.

The Friendship Application

You know the feeling when you go to the supermarket on an empty stomach and end up asking your grown-up for everything you see? But later on, you realise maybe you didn't need all of it and, in fact, you should've been a little bit more thoughtful? Well, Rebels, it can be easy to make that same mistake with our friendships. When we're not intentional about what we want, we can end up accepting less than what we deserve.

If we can supply you with any advice in this chapter, it's to make a list. When we're clear about the things we want, the easier it'll be to get them. On the next page you'll find a list we made together – we're best friends because we check so many things off each other's list. Your list might include other things too, like someone who you can play your favourite sport with or someone who is super creative.

WHAT THE REBELS SAY

"I recently made friends with a girl at school. She was new, and I volunteered to show her around school."
–Charlotte D., 9, Alabama, USA

Friendship Check-list

* **Trust:** What is a friend for if you can't trust them? We think a tell-tale sign of a good friend is someone you can trust. Whether that looks like confiding in them with your biggest secret or knowing without a doubt that they'll be there for you – no questions asked, it's important to trust that they won't let you down.

* **Humour:** Listen, life can be stressful sometimes. We have both found that having a group of friends who know how to lighten the mood – even when things aren't all sunshine and rainbows – is healing. Laughter is the best medicine!

* **Communication:** We've both learned that you can't have a functional (let alone healthy) friendship if you're not communicating your thoughts and feelings. None of us are mind readers. Besides, true love is born from understanding, and how can we ever hope to understand each other if we don't speak up?

* **Kindness:** We have a strict rule in our personal lives: sweeties only. There are some people who think it's cool to be mean, especially on the internet. But we're super wary of anyone who thrives on being cruel, even for the sake of a joke. We've both found that life is much sweeter when you surround yourself with kind people.

Remember, you have the power to create the reality you want to live in. Life is a dream, and you are the dreamer. You are the captain of your fate and the master of your soul. It's up to you to choose the life you want and the people you want to spend it with.

FINDING YOUR PEOPLE

WHAT THE REBELS SAY

"When we're together, the years fall away. Isn't that what matters? To have someone who can remember with you? To have someone who remembers how far you've come?"
—Judy Blume

Right now is such an exciting time in your life. The world is blooming before you. The sky's the limit! You are becoming your own person.

You are entering an era where each experience is suddenly more than a moment in time. It could be the moment you discover something that changes your life. When I was your age, I picked up reading. I always had my nose in a book. Once, in year 6, at the very end of the school year, I spent an entire class period reading while the rest of the class watched a movie. The thing is, I never thought it meant anything. It was just something I did, like brushing my teeth or tying my shoes.

Now, years later, I can say it was *everything*. Reading moulded me in my formative years. More than keeping me entertained, it taught me empathy and expanded my imagination. I built worlds in my head. I wept when characters were outwitted, and I cheered when they won.

Now, being a "big reader" is one of the ways I describe myself. It is a trait I look for in other people. You know, this book was made possible by being a reader. If I hadn't been, I never would have met Sara who, like me, is a big reader. In fact, we met in a book club! The first time we spoke I felt a sudden peace, like I had known her all my life. Like I recognised something of me in her, or her in me.

The Zulu people of South Africa have a name for this feeling. They call it *ubuntu*, which means "humanity." It's a big belief system which says, "You are you because of others." And it's so true. I laugh just like my mum. I bake banana bread exactly the way my best friend taught me. And I've become a more forgiving person since knowing Sara, who is one of the most forgiving people I know.

The people you surround yourself with will shape you. By choosing your friends wisely, you are deciding what kind of person you will grow up to be.

Picture This

Gina has just started year 5, and all her classes are kicking off with a "getting to know you" assignment. Her music teacher asks the class to write an essay about their favourite song and a memory attached to it. Gina is stumped! She loves music. How can she pick just one favourite song?

Gina's parents suggest she think back on special memories and see if any songs come to mind.

Suddenly, it dawns on her. Hands down, her favourite song is "Put Your Records On" by Corinne Bailey Rae. Gina met her best friend, Michaela, when she moved in next door three months ago. It was perfect timing because Gina was also new in town and didn't have any friends yet. They spent the whole summer catching glow-worms, cannon-balling into the pool, and blasting that song.

Most importantly, Michaela didn't make Gina feel embarrassed when she cried over the season finale of their favourite TV show. She'd never felt this close to anyone besides her family before. It's like she and Michaela share the same brain. Sometimes, she swears, they can communicate through looks alone.

Gina ends up writing a heart-felt essay about her favourite song and how it reminds her of her best friend. The assignment was much easier when she had such a wonderful memory to share. Gina is pumped when she gets her grade back – an A+!

The ubuntu philosophy tells us human beings cannot grow alone. In the story above, Michaela showed Gina that supportive, caring friendships help us become our true selves. Remember when Michaela was so cool about Gina crying while watching their favourite TV show? The way Michaela handled that moment made Gina realise she didn't have to be afraid of Michaela making fun of her.

Having Michaela as a friend, inspired Gina to open up and be herself, like a flower blooming. She learned that we can be nourished by laughter and tender care. By friendship bracelets and weekly pep talks. By our friends, one and all.

Finding Common Ground

Rebels, we have a secret to share with you: we have been friends for years, but we could not be more different. If we were planets, we'd be on opposite sides of the galaxy. Camila's would have purple sands and twinkly waters, and there would be no concept of time, ever. Meanwhile, Sara's planet would be green, green, green, and there would be a giant clock to signal when it's time to make art, clean, eat, and sleep. But what makes our friendship so strong is that we complement each other like yin and yang.

In Friendshipland (which we imagine to look like Paradiseland), there's a popular myth that you should only be friends with people who are just like you. But we're here to break the spell and tell you that's a big misunderstanding of

how friendship works. Our lives are like gardens. So many different things can blossom and grow. If you're naturally good at sport and building things with your hands, wouldn't it be cool to be around someone who is imaginative and interested in art? Or if you're an avid book reader, wouldn't it be nice to find a friend who loves movies so you two can trade recommendations?

The world is big and full of interesting people with all different backgrounds and hobbies. If you were only friends with people who were exactly like you, you might find yourself awfully bored in no time. But you don't want to swing too far in the opposite direction and have friends you struggle to talk with.

The secret to friendship isn't being totally alike or even liking all the same things. It's finding common ground in your interests and using your strengths to help each other. When Sara's being hard on herself, Camila reminds her to treat herself with kindness. And if Camila's struggling with her workload, Sara makes her a to-do list so her tasks don't feel overwhelming. Basically, your friendships should feel like a peanut butter & jelly sandwich: two different tastes that become magic when together. Don't limit yourself to an idea of what your friendships should look like. If you do that, you might miss out on some incredible connections.

It's OK that you and your best friend are different! It's even a good thing. Here's a fun diagram that maps out what we have in common, where our interests differ, and how we can learn from each other.

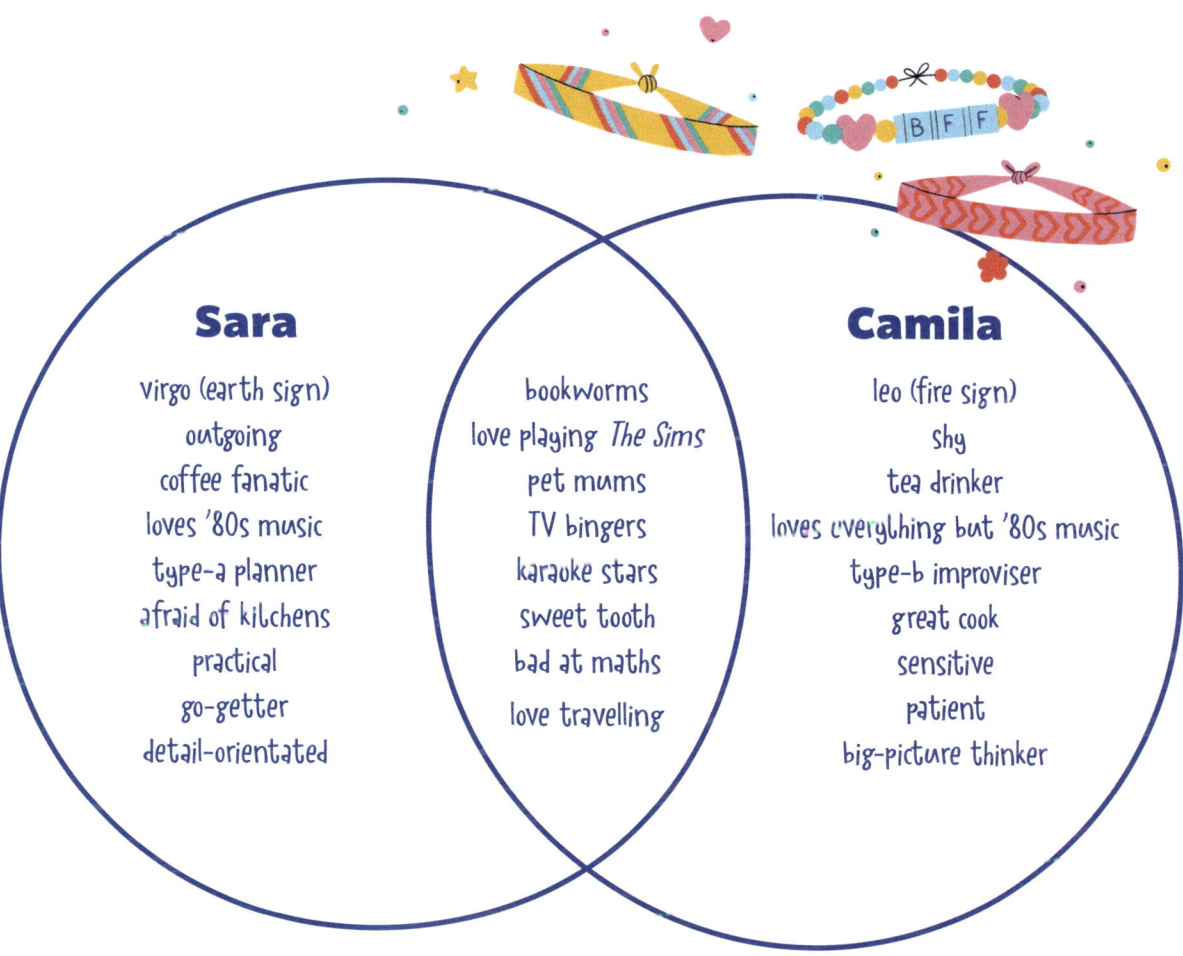

Sara
virgo (earth sign)
outgoing
coffee fanatic
loves '80s music
type-a planner
afraid of kitchens
practical
go-getter
detail-orientated

bookworms
love playing *The Sims*
pet mums
TV bingers
karaoke stars
sweet tooth
bad at maths
love travelling

Camila
leo (fire sign)
shy
tea drinker
loves everything but '80s music
type-b improviser
great cook
sensitive
patient
big-picture thinker

Now, you try it! With your bestie, grab a piece of paper and some markers, crayons, or coloured pencils. Draw two big overlapping circles. Fill in your separate interests and traits in the different circles and the ones you have in common in the middle.

CHOOSING YOUR FRIENDS WISELY

There's a phrase grown-ups sometimes use that goes something like: "They were looking for love in all the wrong places." This can apply to friendships too. Growing up, I was so desperate for any sort of companionship that I didn't stop to think about whether the people I was choosing to be friends with were actually good for me (or even good to me). Now that I have a much better grasp on how to choose the right friends, I'm here to share my hard-earned insights with you.

When I was at secondary school, my first best friend ever was a girl I'll call Taylor. She was blonde, wealthy, and popular. To elevate herself, she used to pick on me in front of the whole school by mocking my appearance, clothes, and interests. Nothing was off-limits. Taylor said it was just teasing, but words have impact and hers were brutal. I was different from her, and she thought that was weird. I was an Asian immigrant. I didn't have the white-picket-fence upbringing she did. I didn't wear the cool brands, and I didn't know the American customs she grew up with. Though we were inseparable, she didn't treat me as an equal.

Looking back, it's clear being friends with Taylor just made me feel bad. And friendships – when fulfilling and real – should never make you feel less than. When Taylor pointed out all of my insecurities on the playground, I became embarrassed to fully be myself. Instead of helping me rise to my full potential, she made me feel small. But it was a hard feeling to pinpoint because of how close we were: her family invited me on vacation, she took me on summer trips, and we spent most weekends together.

Rebels, sometimes it takes getting pricked by a few thorns before we find a rose. I don't miss Taylor, or our friendship, but I do appreciate what it taught me. What I regret most is that, to protect myself from Taylor's barbs, I started being mean as a defence mechanism. I treated others with unwarranted cruelty before they could – hypothetically – hurt me the way she did. I'm not proud of this fact, but I understand it now.

There's the saying that the people we surround ourselves with are a reflection of us and our values. Taylor was a Cool Girl™, but she was a bully. By extension, I started to treat myself and the people around me with the same viciousness I was used to. In the end, my loss of identity wasn't worth the trade-off for proximity to Taylor. But I didn't have that voice of reason then – which is why I hope I can be that for you instead.

Yes, there were dozens of red flags I should have spotted in my friendship with Taylor. But when you're looking at everything through rose-tinted glasses, all those red flags just become flags. Rebels, it's important to move through life with an open heart, but we must keep our heads and intuition with us.

As you embark on this beautiful journey of finding true companionship and friendship, I want you to be smart and not find yourself a Taylor but a Camila.

What Are You Looking For in a Friend?

1. What is your ideal ice-breaker?

   A. Deep conversation: You have no interest in small talk and prefer to dive right into your goals and dreams (just like Camila).
   B. Finding mutual interests: You're a cheerleader for the things you love, whether that's sport, pop stars, fashion, etc. It means the world to you to find someone who shares the same passion for life that you have.
   C. Trying something together: You have a great sense of humour, and you're not afraid to fall on your face. You need a pal who also loves trying new things.

2. What is your biggest weakness?

   A. Playing it safe: Listen, you like what you like. But if you never put yourself out there, you'll miss out on some pretty amazing opportunities. Maybe that's what your new best friend can help you with.
   B. Being indecisive: What to choose, what to choose? There are so many options in the world, and even picking a place to eat can feel daunting. A best friend can help you trust your gut instincts.
   C. Being hot-headed: You act first, think second. Perhaps you can find a bestie who helps balance out your more impulsive side.

3. How would you prefer to spend your weekends?

   A. Catching up on reading: You're on the more introverted side, and you don't need a big production to have a great time.
   B. Going with the flow: You're open to anything, so you prefer to let others decide. Your rule of thumb is saying yes and seeing where life leads you.
   C. An exciting activity (like rock climbing!): You like to seek out new adventures and keep your blood pumping.

4. Who is your hero?

A. **Greta Gerwig:** You aspire to make something just as meaningful and beloved as *Ladybird*, *Little Women*, or *Barbie*.
B. **Frida Kahlo:** Introverted and perceptive, nothing gets by you. You find beauty and inspiration wherever you are.
C. **Beyoncé:** Bold and fearless. Nothing is keeping Beyoncé from living her dreams! You admire her attitude and outlook on life.

5. In a crisis, what do you need?

A. **To be heard:** Sometimes you just need to vent your emotions to a kind ear.
B. **To understand:** Our feelings don't always make sense, so having a friend who can sort them out with you is priceless.
C. **A solution:** You need a bestie who can sprint into the situation with a plan and advice you can count on.

6. What kind of friend are you?

A. **The nurturer:** You're known as the "mum friend." You keep your backpack fully stocked with anything your friends might need.
B. **The dreamer:** You have a unique way of seeing the world! Your friends admire your out-of-the-box thinking and often go to you for advice.
C. **The go-getter:** You take big risks, and you want to live a big life. You often encourage others to branch out a little.

Answers

Mostly As: A Balancing Act

You know who you are, and that's a true gift! But you can be stuck in your ways. You need a friend who will help push you out of your comfort zone – someone who will bring excitement to your life and help you try something new.

Mostly Bs: A Cheerleader

You are uniquely you and that's beautiful. You don't need to find someone who is exactly like you, just someone who gets you. A best friend who will champion you and encourage you to live your dreams no matter what you do.

Mostly Cs: A Partner in Crime

You need someone who can keep up with you and be the other half of your dynamic duo. Your ideal best friend is someone who can appreciate your curiosity and zest for life. At the same time, you need someone who can ground you when you might fly a little too close to the sun.

ASK THE EXPERTS

Rebel Girls just like you sent in excellent questions about making friends. Real-life besties and the authors of this book, Sara Jin Li and Camila Rivera, weigh in below.

> How do you approach new friends?
> —Kylie M., 10, Georgia, USA

With an open heart! Cheesy, I know, but it's true. I don't like to play it cool. I think in order to find true connection, we have to be vulnerable (even when it feels awkward). When approaching someone, I'll usually compliment them or ask them a question – which shows interest in them. It's OK to let people know you want to be friends. Open mouths get fed, Rebels!

Sara Jin Li
Author

How do you decide who would make a good friend?
—Bayleigh D., 10, Oklahoma, USA

Ooooh, this is a bit of a tough one. I think the decision is always a personal one because we all have different needs. Some people feel they need to have hobbies or activities they enjoy in common with their friends. Others might feel that having a different sense of humour is a deal-breaker. Personally, I know someone is a good friend when I feel safe around them. When I can "show them my belly," as I like to say. When I can trust them with the tenderest parts of me and never lose a wink of sleep over it.

Camila Rivera
Author

CHAPTER 2

HOW TO MAKE FRIENDS

Some girls are naturals at making friends. They walk in, light up the room, and everyone is drawn to them like moths to a flame. Other girls are diamonds in the rough. They don't shine as bright right away (but they're just as special). Sometimes, they get overlooked. It's me . . . I'm other girls.

By the time I left secondary school, I had attended two different primary schools, and five different secondary schools. I was constantly moving and had to make new friends every time. I hated it! Every single time! And it was nerve-racking. Every. Single. Time. However, looking back on those experiences, I recognise they shaped me in ways I never had the language for, until now.

WHAT THE REBELS SAY

"I met my best friend through our school's maths class, and we both helped each other through the parts we didn't understand."
—Stella R., 12, Florida, USA

I love people. I love *all* people. I love them funny or serious. I love them tall and round. I love them short and skinny. I love them with their straight smile, and I love them with a cute gap between their front teeth. I love them if I never see them again, and I love them if I see them every Tuesday. And I've

realised the reason why I love people is because I've known so many of them, and each one has shown me things that no one else could.

New experiences are often nerve-racking. Most humans are creatures of habit. We don't like the unknown, and we don't like walking into the dark. Except that's all we've ever done. Rosa Parks refused to give up her seat, and Frida Kahlo picked up a brush to paint away her pain. Neither knew the impact those actions would have. We're all just trying our best. What we do know is that we would never have got this far if we hadn't had each other.

KNOW WHAT YOU'RE BRINGING TO THE FRIENDSHIP

Rebels, it's time for some real talk. You will learn a lot of lessons in life – some good, some bad – and they will often return to this: the amount of love you have for yourself.

What do I mean by that? Well . . .

Say it with me: You! Are! A! Catch! Making new friends can be scary because it's vulnerable. We put so much of ourselves on the line, hoping to make a connection, fearing rejection. Some of us we downplay just how great we are when we're scared. Just about everyone gets insecure and nervous meeting new people – even us! When we're in a room full of strangers, we have to remind ourselves of what we have to offer. If we're struggling with our confidence, we'll call each other for a pep talk. Sometimes before a big project with people we don't know, we'll write down what we love most about ourselves in my journal. For example, Sara really appreciates her sense of humour, and Camila loves how considerate she is. Feel free to try this! Do it right now. We'll wait.

Over the years, we've developed this strategy of treating everyone we meet like they could

> **WHAT THE REBELS SAY**
>
> "Each friend represents a world in us, a world possibly not born until they arrive, and it is only by this meeting that a new world is born."
> —Anaïs Nin

become on of our best friends. And the funny thing is, as we've forced ourselves to go out of our comfort zone, we've actually become less shy about meeting people. We look forward to new social opportunities because we walk into them with the idea that these could be our future friends. It's how we went from being complete strangers to platonic soulmates today!

So, if you're ever feeling hesitant, just remember you are exactly the type of person that someone's hoping to befriend.

Strike Up a Conversation

Use these tips when approaching a potential new friend.

- **Start with a smile.** Did you know that only 7 per cent of communication happens through the words we use? The other 93 per cent is made up of body language and tone of voice – so a smile says a lot. It invites others in. It is a signal that you are someone who would receive them kindly.
- **Give a compliment.** While a smile is a nice place to start, it's totally possible the person you want to get to know is as shy as you are. You don't want to get stuck in a feedback loop of smiling and secretly longing for one of you to speak up. A genuine compliment is a great way to strike up a conversation. You could say something like, "What a cool bracelet! I love the purple beads. Is purple your favourite colour?"
- **Be observant.** If you're like me, you like to take in your surroundings and gather lots of information first. Say the girl sitting next to you has a water bottle covered in stickers of your favourite pop star. You can ask her where she got the stickers and what she thinks of the singer's new album. Now you two have something to talk about.

So You Walk Into a Room...

... and you don't know *anyone*. It could be a new school, a new youth club, or a new sports team. The point is: everyone has already bonded through their shared experience, and you're the odd one out. What do you do?

You walk in with your head held high.

You remember what you have to offer. Go back to your list, if you need to. You are smart and kind and brave. You deserve to be out in the world. You are much too wonderful a person to keep to yourself. Knowing you is a gift! And knowing other people is a pleasure.

By now, we're sure you've had a new kid join your class. If not, the experience is akin to the morning of your birthday. The atmosphere is charged with the delicious excitement of a perfect surprise. When our class was expecting a new student, we'd ask each other, "Will they be funny? Adventurous? Will they teach us new things?" It usually doesn't occur to anyone that they would be anything other than a friend.

That's what everyone is thinking when you walk into a room and you don't know anyone. Remember that.

Still, it's scary. It can feel like if you say one wrong thing, then *poof*! The spell is broken. It's after midnight and, suddenly, everyone knows you're a pumpkin. Here's the thing: that is false. The magic doesn't come at you, it comes *from* you. So don't be afraid to be your authentic self.

Time for a Confidence Boost

These tips can help you feel strong and ready to put yourself out there.

* **Affirmations:** It's important to build yourself up before you enter a new environment. A friend of ours likes to write compliments to herself in the mirror with a removable marker so she sees them every time she gets ready. A character on my favourite TV show stretches herself out as big as possible and sets her body in power poses. Whatever works for you!

    Doing your affirmations in the shower or bath can be very effective. Water can be healing for many people. Say your affirmations while you imagine all of your insecurities washing away. Try this one: "I am smart. I am capable. I light up every room."

* **Self! Care!:** We're at our most confident when we feel good, so ask yourself, "What makes me feel like my best self?" After a stressful week, we love doing our nails. A little nail polish can go a long way. We also like to take long walks outside. We have an inside joke that human beings are really just complicated houseplants. A little sun, a little water, and we're all charged up and ready to face the world.

* **Ask for help:** Our friends and family can be the best source of confidence boosts. We can be our own worst critics. It's the magnifying-glass effect. You're so zoomed-in on your own experience that you're missing the bigger picture. Asking your bestie (or sibling or grown-up) to remind you of your amazing qualities is a great way to improve your mood. Plus, it's a sweet little exercise in asking for help.

I am smart.
I am capable.
I light up every room.

The Secret to Going from Friendly to Friends

Rebels, English really *is* my second language, so I know exactly what I'm talking about when I say that striking up conversations does feel a bit like speaking in tongues. It can feel like you've suddenly become overly aware of your body, your clothes, how you're standing, and your breath (does it stink? Why didn't you suck a sweet after lunch?). You might feel like an alien pretending to be human. Everything is awkward and terrible and forced, and time's going so slow, and oh no, you think you're sweating a little on your upper lip – gross! – and why oh why won't the ground open up and swallow you alive?

Fortunately, and unfortunately, there isn't a script for every social situation. But here's a little-known secret I didn't find out until later in life: whatever you think you're doing, however embarrassed and small and weird you might feel, the other person is probably feeling the same way. You're worried that you sound funny? They're hoping their deodorant

is working. We exist so much in our own heads that sometimes we forget that everyone else is nervous too.

Making friends – the long-lasting, fill-your-heart-with-warmth kind – isn't about saying or doing the right thing all the time. It has nothing to do with putting on a facade or showing only the shiniest parts of yourself. Sure, it would be grand if we could be polished all the time, but is that realistic? No! It doesn't even sound fun. Making friends is about letting the silliness in you see the silliness in them. It's about taking all the mismatched parts of yourself and finding a place in each other to call home.

Your friends are going to be the people who see you at your worst and your best. Rebels, you *have* to let them in. Let yourself be cringe! Aren't you tired of playing it cool? Aren't we all?

Most people you meet want to make friends. Some of us have welcomed this and are standing before you, arms outstretched, waiting to be embraced. Others are still a bit shy, hesitant to fully let themselves want it. I won't lie to you, it may be uncomfortable in the beginning. The road from meeting someone to becoming their friend is paved with good intentions and awkward ice-breakers. But keep trying. Follow up on plans and be proactive about seeing them, learning more about them, and opening up about yourself.

Good friendships rarely (if ever!) drop in our laps. If a girl in your class is wearing the T-shirt of a band you like, ask her if she wants to listen to the new album together. If you're struggling in maths class, see if one of your classmates wants to study together. When we open our eyes to possibilities, we'll see there's a world full of them.

First Friend Dates

Looking for an activity to do with a new friend? Here are some of our top recommendations.

* **Go to a movie or a school play.** Not only will it be a great way to gauge each other's tastes and opinions, you'll have plenty to talk about afterwards. Some of my favourite nights out with my closest friends involve watching a movie and dissecting it afterwards. Time will fly, trust me.

* **Try something new for the both of you.** What's more bold than dipping your toes into the unknown? This can be anything: roller-skating, hiking, karaoke, etc. You'll always share a special memory.

* **Do some window shopping.** You don't need unlimited funds to have a good time. You just need good company and imagination! Take a stroll around your local bookshop, or visit your favourite store and pretend you're buying something for your future wedding. It's fun to play and make believe.

* **Have a picnic at the park.** It's been scientifically proven that a little bit of sunshine goes a long way. Prep your favourite snacks, grab some sunscreen, and head to the park to enjoy a nice time of fresh air and good company.

BIRDS OF A FEATHER FLOCK TOGETHER

Words to live by: you find your friends where you find your joy.

Let's say you grew up camping with your family every summer, and you love nature. Your grandpa taught you how to do bird calls, and you're getting really good at discerning between the different species. Maybe you should consider joining your local Girlguiding unit. It's a sure way to find friends who enjoy the outdoors as much as you do.

That's just one example. If you love gymnastics, you'll likely meet some great friends at the a gymnastics class. If you're more into art, we can pretty much guarantee you'll find someone you hit it off with in an art class. Our point is: think about what you love to do, do more of it, and you'll be surprised how quickly you make like-minded friends.

Picture This

Dani has just moved to a new town, and she's bored. The most exciting thing to happen in the three weeks she's been there is the new bird's nest constructed on the tree branch right outside her window.

She used to have so much to do back home! She and her best friend loved roller-skating. They had a standing arrangement every second Saturday of the month to meet at the local park and skate together. Now she spends her days roller-skating alone in her driveway.

One night, Dani has a vivid dream. She's in a lighthouse on a stormy night. It's cold and dark, and Dani is scared because she's all alone. Just when she thinks the storm is going to sweep her away, a falling star crashes into the lighthouse, landing in her hands.

Somehow, she knows exactly what she needs to do. Dream-Dani sticks the star in the place the lighthouse beam should be, illuminating the horizon. That's when she notices a ship appear. Then another. And then another.

Before long, the entire horizon is lit up by ship lights heading towards her, like the answer to her call.

Dani wakes up feeling much better. The dream helped her realise that while her sad feelings are valid, wallowing in them is keeping her from finding new friends. Inspired, she starts researching roller-skating clubs in her area and finds out the local youth club hosts one every week! Pretty soon, Dani is a regular at the meet-ups, where she meets a bunch of friends.

When you find people who love the same thing you do, it's a good indicator you have other things in common too. However, the only way to find people with similar interests is to put yourself out there.

Sure, Dani was nervous to start over, but more than anything, she was disappointed to leave her life behind. She had worked hard to put together an awesome group of girls who enjoyed the same hobby. It had felt really special – how could she ever hope to capture that feeling again?

To be honest, Rebels, you can't. The special thing about friendships is that they're all wonderfully unique. What you have with one person you'll never have with anyone else. It might be similar, but it'll never truly be the same. The point is not to chase that "perfect" feeling, but to accept that every positive feeling is perfect because it is unique.

So, no matter how hard it gets, go out and find your joy! Somewhere, there is a friendship waiting to be discovered. There is a flock waiting for its newest feathered friend.

43

GETTING TO KNOW EACH OTHER

Making new friends is incredibly beautiful, but it can also be inescapably awkward. And it doesn't change with age, either. A friend of ours moved from Brazil to Texas in her mid-20s, and she will be the first person to tell you how hard it is to make friends as an adult. So, in an ironic way, we're all in this together. It's nerve-racking because getting to know someone requires us to let our guard down and show someone what excites us, what gives us the creeps, and why we are the way we are.

It's a lot!

Sometimes it even feels tedious. If you're someone who moves around a lot, you've probably experienced the rinse-and-repeat of having to introduce yourself over and over. It's tiring, right? Anyone who has been a new kid has vivid flashbacks of standing up in front of the classroom and introducing themselves to 20-plus kids who already know each other. When I was the new kid, I remember a knot of fear tightening in my belly. *What if no one likes me?* I thought. *What if this is the beginning of the rest of my life, eating lunch alone, being friendless?* Even though all those fears were just in my head, they felt all too real in the moment.

But the truth is, we won't ever be proven wrong unless we try. To make friends, we have to be brave.

Dial-a-Friend: Malia Pyles

US actor Malia Pyles is bigger than life on *Pretty Little Liars: Original Sin* as Mouse, but IRL, she knows exactly what it's like to struggle making new friends. After some trial and error, she's figured out a few tried-and-true tricks.

Finding friendships that stick can be tough, and there's no perfect formula on how to do it. But with some effort, it's certainly possible and totally worth it. After moving to a big city, I made it my goal to find my chosen family. And I have! A great place to start is to do things or go places where you feel your individual self shine and sparkle. This could be playing a sport, taking an art class, volunteering, or just frequenting a local bookshop. A shared space has the potential to be a shared path.

I know talking to new people can be scary, but start with just one person. Ask them about their journey, and I'm sure you'll find someone with an open mind and heart to have adventures with. Also, remember: you and what you have to offer to a friendship are worthwhile. For example, sharing your favourite food, place, or TV show with someone new can be a gift they didn't previously have. Sara asked me to go to a play, which was perfect because I didn't have any friends at the time who were interested in theatre like I was. She had, without knowing, granted a very special wish of mine. Our friendship blossomed. The truth is: most people are looking for friends. It just takes one brave moment to create a relationship that will last a lifetime.

45

Books to Bond Over with Your Bestie(s)

We all know that friendships are worth the risk of putting ourselves out there. There's no greater reward! But . . . well, sometimes we could use extra encouragement. Luckily, authors everywhere have been documenting the magic of friendship for ages. And just to prove that it never ever goes out of style, we rounded up our favourite books about friendship. Read them solo, with your bestie, or with some new friends.

* **Bridge to Terabithia by Katherine Paterson:**

    A classic. Neighbours and schoolmates Jesse Aarons and Leslie Burke strike up a friendship and create an entire kingdom from their imagination in their forest backyard.

* **Number the Stars by Lois Lowry:** A real tear-jerker. This coming-of-age tale is set during World War II and follows Annemarie Johansen and Ellen Rosen, two 10-year-old best friends who find themselves facing impossible odds. Bring your tissues!

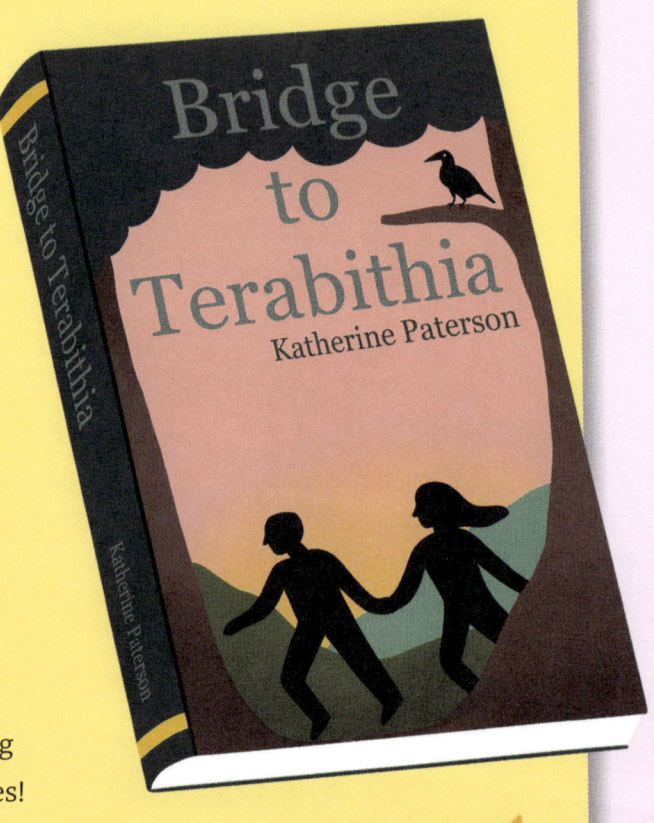

* **Holes by Louis Sachar:** When Stanley Yelnats is sent to a correctional camp for convicts, he learns a lot about himself while striking up unexpected and unconventional friendships.

* **The Sisterhood of the Travelling Pants by Ann Brashares:** The perfect summer read. Four best friends embark on their own summer adventures but stay in touch by mailing back and forth a thrifted pair of jeans that magically fit all of them perfectly. You can read the entire series if you don't want to stop at one. The movie versions are great for sleepovers.

* **The School for Good and Evil by Soman Chainani:** A must-read series. Best friends Sophie and Agatha get swept up in magic but must counter their differences when they are sorted into different schools for fairy-tale heroes and villains. If you like the book, you'll definitely like the movie.

Where Will You Meet Your Next Best Friend?

1. **What hobby would you like to pick up?**
   A. You have a knack for music . . . playing an instrument!
   B. Something crafty, like knitting or scrapbooking
   C. Learning a new language, of course
   D. Mountain biking

2. **What is your go-to karaoke song?**
   A. "Love Story" by Taylor Swift
   B. "Mamma Mia" by ABBA
   C. "Part of Your World" from *The Little Mermaid*
   D. "Roar" by Katy Perry

3. **On a big car ride, how are you killing time?**
   A. Watching a documentary
   B. Messaging my bestie
   C. Reading a new biography
   D. Listening to a game on the radio

4. **How would your loved ones describe you?**
   A. A busy bee
   B. The ultimate cheerleader
   C. Someone who loves to learn new things
   D. A real go-getter

5. **Which career sounds most interesting to you?**
   A. Party planner
   B. Therapist
   C. College professor
   D. Professional athlete

6. **It's summer vacation. What's on your bucket list?**
   A. Finishing your library's summer reading challenge
   B. Going to the beach with my best friends
   C. Starring in the community theatre's play
   D. Going to a sports camp

Answers

Mostly As: An After-School Extracurricular

You love to keep busy, so it makes sense that your new friend will be someone who is passionate about their hobbies too. Don't be afraid to branch out and try your hand at something new. Joining an after-school club – like debating or the football team – is a great way to meet new people. And you'll have a new friend to cheer you on.

Mostly Bs: Through a Mutual Friend

Your new best friend could be just around the corner. And you don't know it yet, but you might already have a lot in common. This is your sign to go to that acquaintance's birthday party or that overnight trip with your childhood best friend. They just might introduce you to someone awesome – and soon you'll be inseperable.

Mostly Cs: In Your Favourite Class

Great news: the place to find your next best friend is somewhere you go five days a week: school! Sometimes a new friend is someone you've never met before. And sometimes, they're someone you already know. Pay attention to who in your class catches your eye. Maybe they have the coolest notebooks or love the same subjects you do. It's time to go from friendly to friends.

Mostly Ds: At a Sports Match

Nothing excites you as much as a close match of your favourite sport. Sure, you might lose your voice on occasion from cheering so much, but it's totally worth it. It only makes sense that your new friend is just as enthusiastic about the game. The next time you're in the stands (or even on the field), look to see who's around and having the time of their life too.

ASK THE EXPERTS

Talking to new people and navigating social dynamics can be tricky, so we reached out to psychotherapist Alexandra Vaccaro and school counsellor Beth Lucas to share their insights.

> What do I do if someone doesn't want to be my friend?
> —McKenzie M., 9, Maryland, USA

It is hard when someone doesn't want to be your friend. Hurt feelings are no fun! That being said, if someone doesn't want to spend time with you and treat you kindly, I think it is best to move on. Focus on the people who appreciate all of the positive qualities that you have and spend your time building relationships with them.

**Beth Lucas
School Counsellor**

How can I get past being scared to speak to new people?
—Morgan T., 8, Texas, USA

Like anything new or unfamiliar to us, meeting new people can be nerve-racking. A great way to work on conquering your worries is by practising how you would approach a social situation with someone you feel comfortable with, like a grown-up. Talking through a little script of a situation you are nervous about (also known as role-playing) can help you feel more confident and less worried. If acting things out isn't your thing, you can just talk through what you're going to say or what things may come up during a particular social event with your trusted adult. When we have a plan for how to handle an interaction, it can make it a lot less scary.

**Alexandra Vaccaro
Psychotherapist**

CHAPTER 3
BEING A GOOD FRIEND

When it comes to friendship, quality is always, always better than quantity. I used to want to be the most popular girl in my school, but I learned the hard way that having the most friends didn't necessarily make *me* the best friend. What I value now is different from what I did then because, at the end of the day, I just want my friends to be as loved as possible. It doesn't matter that I don't have 100 friends, it matters that the 10 I consider my close friends know I'm there for them through thick and thin.

It's not just about making friends, it's about being a good friend too.

And maybe here's something no one tells you: it's not always easy. Like any relationship, there might be rough patches and ups and downs. Sometimes we even have to practise how to be a good friend through trial and error. But the more we show up in our friendships, again and again, the more we strengthen the bonds we have. Being a good friend isn't about being perfect all the time - it's about leading with love, apologising when we mess up, and being gracious and generous in return.

As we dive into this chapter, remember this: love is not only a feeling, it is an action. Taking action to show you care could mean helping your friend study for a subject she's struggling in, even when you'd rather be watching TV. It could mean showing up to their softball game even if it's chilly and drizzly out. It could mean treating them with gentle hands, even when they're in a grumpy mood. Do you see that word "*even*"? Supporting your friends means loving them, even when it's new or hard. Little things like these go a long way towards making your friendships richer.

THERE'S NO FRIENDSHIP WITHOUT SUPPORT

Have you heard of the saying, "Sharing is caring?" Most of us learned it when we were younger. When we care about someone, we want to give them what we have. One of our favourite ways to show love to our friends is by giving them something, whether it's flowers or a book that reminds us of them. But it's not just about the physical stuff – friendship is also about sharing each other's joy and interests.

Fun fact: one of Camila's favourite sayings is, "If you like it, I love it." Sara knows Camila will support her in all her pursuits, from a new hobby to a career change.

Without support, it's tough for any relationship to last. You deserve to feel like your friends are cheering you on! One of our best friends, Gina, is going to be a lawyer, which could not be more different than the creative path we're on. But we listen to one another talk about our goals, our work, and what we hope to accomplish in our fields. It doesn't matter that we're not always interested in the same things. Years of friendship later, Gina will still send us things – memes, articles, even physical gifts – that remind her of us, just to tell us we're on her mind.

Friendship isn't about finding the perfect person who matches everything we're into. It's about finding the people who will stand by you, no matter what.

Dial-a-Friend: Madison McLaughlin

When we think about people we cherish, our good friend Madison McLaughlin is the first to come to mind. As an actor (you might've seen her in the shows *Arrow*, *Teen Wolf*, or *Supernatural*) and the internet's big sister, Madison knows how to make people feel loved. We asked her to share her favourite ways to show people she loves and supports them. Here's what she had to say.

1. Texting a friend something as simple as "This song reminds me of you!" can be a great conversation starter. It shows you're paying attention to their taste.

2. If a friend is in a band, music lessons, or sport, ask when they have a recital, show, or game you can attend. People who are on the shy side might be too embarrassed to invite people, so make sure your friends know you want to show up for them.

3. If a friend has a different background than you, ask to help them make a favourite childhood recipe. It's a fun way to learn about their culture and how they grew up, while also getting to share a meal together.

4. Design a cute card – it doesn't have to be their birthday for them to enjoy a handwritten note. Something as simple as "Just thinking of you!" or "You're the best!" Jazz it up with scratch-and-sniff stickers or dried flowers from your garden.

HOW TO COMMUNICATE EFFECTIVELY

You know what's interesting, Rebels? As I look back on my friendships (old, new, and current), I've been realising that the source of most of the fights, falling outs, and hurt feelings aren't because of any Big (capital B) thing. In fact, most of the difficult periods in my relationships begin with small miscommunications. Maybe we didn't say how we really felt, maybe we assumed something that wasn't totally true, or maybe we didn't listen as much as we should have.

Picture This

Millie and Nathalie have been best friends since year 4. They've always done *everything* together. But lately things feel different. Nathalie didn't think it was a big deal at first. So what if she's into ballet and Millie is crazy about softball? They could still pretty much read each other's minds . . . right?

Nathalie learns the answer to that question when she and Millie get into their first fight ever. She heads home crying.

After a fresh wave of tears subsides, her mother asks her to calmly recount the conversation they had.

It turns out, Nathalie wanted Millie to come on their family beach trip, but it was the same week as Millie's championship softball game. This was the third time Millie had reminded Nathalie about the date, but Nathalie had forgotten about it.

Nathalie's mum points out that not paying attention once was an honest mistake, but twice might have given Millie the impression she didn't care. Nathalie hadn't even considered that. She was too busy focusing on the last thing Millie had said: "FINE! I don't want to go on your stupid trip anyway!" After a warm hug from her mother, she feels like she's ready to talk to Millie and smooth things over.

When they get together at Nathalie's house, they each apologise. Millie admits that she didn't mean what she had said. She loves their summer trips. Millie just didn't want to say what she was really thinking: she wanted Nathalie to be there to support her at the game and was hurt that Nathalie didn't seem to care at all. Nathalie apologises for forgetting the date and assures her that she'll be there to cheer her best friend on. Nathalie's mum agrees with the plan and moves the family beach trip to the weekend after Millie's big game.

Talk sounds easy, but it's actually really, really hard. There's a lot that goes into healthy communication, and you may have to put extra effort into being understanding. At the end of the day, you have to know that – no matter how much you've hurt each other's feelings – it is not you versus your friend. It is you and your friend versus The Problem. If Nathalie and Millie hadn't realised that, they might have let themselves grow apart. Instead, the two communicated their feelings and realised that the love and respect they had for each other was still there, and that it would allow them to work through their problems together.

So tackle the problem together. Are you understanding each other well? Are you respecting each other? If not, ask yourselves what you need from the other in order to feel valued. No one is a mind reader – and no one is perfect. I've made my fair share of mistakes too. What matters is not what you did when you were at your worst. What matters is how you handled it afterwards, and how you made it right. It won't always be easy, but it will always be worth it.

WHAT THE REBELS SAY

"Last season at lacrosse I learned to be a good teammate by helping the other girls learn the game. And I made a new friend out of it!"
—Reese A., 10, Georgia, USA

What Would You Do?

Sometimes it's helpful to imagine how you would handle sticky friendship situations. Give the ones below a think!

Scenario 1: Brady was excited when she learned her parents signed her up for a summer trip. Of course she was going to miss her best friend Isla – but they promised to write to each other every day. Brady was confident nothing would change. Except . . . as time went on, Isla and Brady wrote to each other less and less. It turns out that a new girl moved in next door while Brady was gone and Isla had spent the summer getting close to her. Brady is feeling replaced. She wonders if she should tell her bestie how she feels?

Scenario 2: Sophia's been having a hard time with her friend Carly. It feels like she can't get a word in edgeways without Carly snapping at her. Sophia tries to be patient with her. She even does her breathing exercises like her mum taught her, but enough is enough! One day at school, Sophia ends up losing her cool on Carly, and now they're not even speaking. What is Sophia supposed to do when *clearly* she's the victim in this scenario? Should she be the one to say sorry anyway?

Scenario 3: Recently, Gwen's friend Abby has started to take her belongings without her permission. It's usually small things – like the last sweet treat from her lunchbox or her favourite hair clip. Gwen tries not to sweat the small stuff. But when the teacher surprises her with a pop quiz, Gwen notices her lucky pencil is missing. She's so nervous while taking the quiz that she can't focus. At lunch, she notices her pencil behind Abby's ear. Gwen decides to speak up for herself, but her friend laughs at her! "You really believe this pencil is lucky?" Abby says. Suddenly, Gwen is doubting herself. Maybe it wasn't such a big deal?

Lead With Love

Sometimes our emotions can feel bigger than our bodies. They can cloud our judgement and can prompt us to believe untrue things like, "My friend doesn't want to be friends with me anymore," or "My friend is intentionally hurting me." In the scenarios on the previous pages, we learned that Brady is hesitant to embrace a change in dynamic between her and Isla because she feels there might not be enough room for someone new. There might not be enough love for *everyone*. What you need to remember, Rebels, is that love is a renewable resource.

After a long conversation with her mum, Brady decides to give Isla's new friend a chance and discovers they absolutely love the same book series. Now Brady has a new friend too. The three of them spend the rest of the summer chasing glow-worms and talking until they fall asleep trading messages on their group text.

But what about when other people aren't leading with love? Sophia's been having a really tough time since the big fight. Carly hasn't reached out, so she obviously doesn't care . . . right? Well, not everything is black and white. Sophia realises this when she later hears Carly's parents are getting a divorce. Suddenly, Carly's short fuse makes sense. In the same way that Sophia found it difficult to confront her friend about her comments, her friend found it difficult to talk about her feelings. Especially when her feelings felt bigger than her body. After a lot of apologies (from both sides) and a few tears, Sophia and Carly are better friends than ever.

Sometimes, when we communicate our feelings, we are received with care. Other times, like in Gwen's situation, our friends can downplay our feelings. It might have been just a pencil to Abby, but it was lucky because Gwen *believed* in it. A true friend would never laugh at our beliefs. Our friends should be our biggest supporters, and Gwen's friend Abby wasn't being very supportive. After a reassuring pep talk with her best friend, Gwen knows that while Abby isn't obligated to believe in the same things, she does need to respect them.

R-E-S-P-E-C-T, Find Out What It Means to ME!

Listen, Rebels, I'm an adult, and I still struggle with setting boundaries. I grew up thinking true love is unconditional, but it's not. Love is sustainable when it's conditional and for a reason. This is what setting boundaries is. It is saying "I love you endlessly as *long* as you're kind to me. As long as you respect me. As long as you value me. As long as . . ."

The tricky thing about boundaries is we don't know what boundaries to set until we need them. But that's OK – the more we learn, the easier it gets. Here's an example: let's say one of your friends tells the whole lunch table they caught you falling asleep and drooling in class. It's not your fault your new puppy woke you up five times last night! And, sure, they were just joking around, but it was more

hurtful to you than funny. You would never embarrass a friend like that. You've now realised that teasing that embarrasses you is something you don't like. You can gently tell your friend that, while you know it was a joke, you're sensitive to teasing and ask her to please keep that in mind.

Or maybe it's a smaller betrayal. For instance, it seems like a given that your new school friend would sleep over at your house. It's like a bestie rite of passage – you don't invite just anyone to a sleepover! So when she says no, and it's a *firm* no, you feel a little deceived. Like, are you really friends or aren't you? What's the big deal?

This is why communication is important. Maybe she isn't allowed to have sleepovers. That is a boundary that she and her parents have agreed upon. While it may disappoint you, it still needs to be respected – the same way you would want her to respect any boundaries you agreed to with your parents. In this case, the way you can respect the boundary is by not bringing up sleepovers. Instead you could invite your friend over for just the movie and ice-cream sundae part of the night.

The point is: we won't always love each other well, but we can always try. Part of that effort is rooted in constant communication about what we need to feel respected (and vice versa). Boundaries aren't punishment. They're our way of telling our friends how to support and love us. It takes a lot of guts to advocate for yourself, but your friendships will be better off for it in the long run.

HOW TO HELP A FRIEND THROUGH A HARD TIME

No matter how old we get, life never stops its trials and tribulations. You might have a hard time with a certain school subject, or maybe you and your sibling start butting heads more often. As wonderful as our existence can be, there's no denying that it can be challenging. We wish we could tell you that life will be easier the more grown up you get, but the truth is that we just learn how to handle our hardships better.

It's inevitable that our family members, like our friends, will struggle too. Those are times when they'll lean on people (like you!) to get back up. And when they do, remember that no one expects you to be an expert in handling hardship. Sometimes, through no fault of your own, the problems your friends face are so much bigger than you can tackle on our own. You might find yourself feeling anxious or frustrated that there's not more you can do to help your friend – and that's completely natural, Rebels.

Sometimes it's the little things, like keeping up in science class. Sometimes it's the real Big Things, like losing a grandparent. And a lot of times, we have to learn the hard lesson that we cannot take away our friends' hurt, no matter how much we want to. The most we can do is support them and let them know we're there for them. It may seem small, but trust us when we say that having a friend by your side during the worst of times is the greatest gift you can give.

Crisis Cheat Sheet

We have suffered through all of the moments – awkward, sad, confusing – so that you don't have to, Rebels. Here is a sweet little cheat sheet to refer to when an uncomfortable situation comes up and you don't know how to respond.

1. **Scenario**: Your bestie totally bombed her maths quiz.

   Response: "Ugh, that stinks. Why don't we plan to study together for the next one?"

2. **Scenario**: Your friend is feeling down about not making the sports team.

   Response: "I'm so sorry you didn't make the team. This doesn't change the fact that you're an amazing athlete. Keep practising! I know your time will come."

3. **Scenario**: A classmate confides in you about their social anxiety.

   Response: "Sometimes I get self-conscious too. Taking deep, calming breaths usually helps me. If that doesn't work, let's decide on a signal. That way, I will know when to come over and help you out."

4. **Scenario**: Your little sister is nervous about starting a new school.

   Response: "You are so smart and funny. Anyone would be lucky to know you. You'll make friends in no time." Then, take some time to read through chapter two of this book together.

5. **Scenario**: Your bestie is feeling overwhelmed with homework, sports practise, and chores at home – it's all too much!

   Response: "Do you need to cry? Scream?" If yes, hold space for them to have their moment. If not, then proceed with: "Let's list everything out in order of priority and tackle one thing at a time. Is there anything I can help you with?"

In 2020, Sara was going through a hard time. She had just moved across the country and was struggling to find a direction in her life. She met Tess, and it was like a prayer had been answered. The two had an immediate connection and were able to be vulnerable with one another. When Sara had big feelings she didn't know what to do with, Tess reminded her that she didn't have to carry them alone. Like a good friend, Tess validated Sara's emotions – and talked them through with her until Sara felt better.

Similarly, Tess was having a bad time at work because she wasn't able to focus. Sara realised Tess might have ADHD (attention deficit hyperactivity disorder) and brought it up with her. Later, Tess was able to see a psychiatrist, who confirmed the diagnosis. Now Tess has the tools she needs to succeed and a forever friend by her side.

Paging the Expert

Sometimes there's no clear answer on what we can do to help our loved ones in need. We asked Beth Lucas, school counsellor, for some advice about helping our friends when they're feeling down. Here's what she had to say.

1. Be present. Sometimes you don't even have to say anything. There is power and healing in knowing you are not alone.

2. Listen. Many times people just want to know that someone else hears them and understands what they are going through.

3. Ask your friends what they need. Sometimes what we think a person needs and what they actually need are very different. By saying something like, "I care about you and can see you are having a hard time. What can I do to help?" you are letting them know you are available and willing to help.

THE INS AND OUTS OF SECRET-KEEPING

We have always thought that a good secret is like a good dessert: it's fun to indulge! Whenever something silly or dramatic or embarrassing happens to us (more often than you'd think), we immediately race to FaceTime each other. Secrets are sacred in friendships – we all have them. But like when you have too much of anything – like chocolate cake (remember that scene in *Matilda*?) – it doesn't feel good after a while.

Yes, secrets are a natural part of friendship. There are always going to be those sweet moments that are precious between you and a friend, shared with no one else. But what if keeping a secret means hurting someone? It can be hard to find the line between harmless secret-keeping and dangerous secret-keeping. And a lot of times, we don't know which is what until it's too late.

We can't lie, Rebels, it's confusing. Even when your intentions are good, it can be tricky to know whether you're helping a friend or accidentally hurting them. To help, we made a check-list of times when it's OK to keep a secret and when it may be time to bring in help. But no matter what, remember this rule of thumb: you should always feel comfortable sharing things with the trusted adults in your life (even if it is *technically* a secret).

Keep It

- Your bestie's parents are getting divorced, but she's not ready to tell anyone else.

- Your bestie has a new crush on the captain of the football team.

- Your bestie is exploring or questioning their sexuality or gender identity.

- Your bestie is thinking about trying something new – like a hobby or extracurricular activity – even if it means quitting something else they've been doing forever.

- Your bestie got some seriously bad news about their health, but no one at school knows.

Spill It

- One of your bestie's other friends is pressuring them into doing something they don't want to do.

- Your bestie has been thinking about or engaging in self-harm.

- Your bestie has a new friend who is a bad influence. Together, they've been doing risky things and breaking rules.

- Your bestie has been experiencing harassment on social media and it's making them depressed.

Bottom line: Whatever secret your friends are asking you to keep shouldn't make you feel uncomfortable or endanger them. No one wants to be a tell-tale – trust us, we get it – but if your friends are at risk in any way, it's best to tell an adult like a parent, teacher, or school counsellor.

Respect O-meter

Consider this quiz an ice-breaker exercise for you and a friend. There never seems to be a good time to talk about the *R* word, and who wants to be responsible for bringing down the vibe? Still, it's an important chat to have. Try as we might, we're not mind readers. That's why having an open dialogue (this means a continuous conversation) about expectations – and setting boundaries around those expectations – is the ideal way to make sure your relationships are in good shape. So grab your bestie and get cosy. Clear your heads. Take three deep breaths. Let yourself ponder each question and, when in doubt, listen to your heart.

1. What are some ways you like to show respect? How do you like to receive it? (Example: holding the door open, saying please and thank you, listening attentively.)

2. True or false: Respect also means respecting your own boundaries, and saying "NO" when you're uncomfortable.

3. Can you disagree with a friend and still be respectful? How do you politely express your feelings?

4. Your teacher is out sick for the week. You know what that means... substitute teacher! Do you join in on the class clownery or try and make your teacher proud?

5. **You accidentally knock over your friend's science-fair project. You know they've been working on it super hard for weeks. How do you handle the situation? (Alternatively: If it were your project, how would you want the situation handled?)**

6. **Your friend is picked to read aloud to the class. They begin, but it's clear they're having some trouble. The rest of your classmates are starting to giggle. How do you react?**

7. **Your bestie becomes obsessed with a new TV show … and you absolutely hate it. Normally, this wouldn't be a big deal, but she won't stop going on about it. How do you kindly express your feelings?**

8. **The fair is in town, and your group of friends decide to go. Everyone is having so much fun. Or so you think … until you notice a new girl from school looking left out. What do you do?**

Answers

There's no answer key to this one. Instead, let your bestie be your answer key. Are your answers more or less in the same vein as each other's? If so, you're doing just fine! If not, that's absolutely OK. The good thing about needing to improve is that it means you have plenty of room to grow.

ASK THE EXPERTS

Alexandra and Sara know a thing or two about being a good friend. Check out the answers to questions Rebel Girls submitted on this topic below.

> How should I comfort a friend when they are sad or hurt?
> —Zooey P., 12, Toronto, Canada

The best way to comfort a friend who is sad or upset is by being present. Be sure to listen to them and meet them where they are at that moment. If they don't feel like talking, let them know you totally understand and that you are available to just be there so they aren't alone. You could suggest watching their favourite movie or taking a walk in the park. Letting a friend know that if they need you, you will be there is the greatest comfort you can give during a difficult time.

Alexandra Vaccaro
Psychotherapist

> Besides buying presents, what are some things I can do to show my friends I care?
> —Alice N., 10, Brighton, England

Caring is in the action, not the gift! I love to spend time with my friends, so I appreciate the simple things like going for a walk, having a picnic in the park, or going to the library (which is always free). Your friends will know you care when you ask them how they're doing, remember their interests, and join them in activities they love. Anyone can give a present, but only you can give the gift of yourself (cheesy, but true).

Sara Jin Li
Author

CHAPTER 4
DIFFERENT TYPES OF FRIENDSHIPS

Besties, I'm going to let you in on a secret. No one can be *everything* we need them to be. More often than not, our best friends are on the same page as us. It's easy to assume that whatever you like, your friends will like too! This isn't always the case, though.

For instance, while Sara is definitely my movie premiere friend and my bookshop-hopping friend, she is absolutely *not* my passenger-seat DJ friend. She may have great taste in books and art, but our taste in music could not be more different. (Love you, Sara!)

The point is: it's unfair for any of us to put our friends in boxes. It doesn't leave them any room to change or surprise you. If I wasn't open to learning about Sara's music taste, then I would have missed out on all the artists she listens to that I *do* like. I would have never awoken to the genius of Olivia Rodrigo.

> **WHAT THE REBELS SAY**
>
> "I make new friends everywhere I go. I smile and introduce myself. I make friends in the library, at the park, at dance class, even at the supermarket."
> —Rosie D., 7, Indiana, USA

I value the differences between my friends and me so much. I actively seek out friendships with people who are different from me because I want to hear different opinions. I want my understanding of a situation to be stretched to its limit. Ubuntu, remember? We understand ourselves more deeply through our relationships with other people. If you want to be a fully realised person, Rebels, you have to learn to not only accept the contrast between your life and your friends' lives, but you have to learn to celebrate it too.

FINDING LOVE IN A HOPELESS PLACE

In the winter of 2020, from other sides of the country, we made the spontaneous decision to join a book club online. We've always been big readers, but neither of us really had the time to enjoy it like we used to. When the world started shutting down, we found ourselves feeling very isolated and returned to the one thing that's always brought us comfort in bleak times: burying our heads in a good book! We were two strangers who found each other through this shared hobby. As our conversations progressed from what we were reading to what we were doing, the wee flame of friendship was slowly but surely kindling.

It's unfathomable to us to think that without that book club, we would have never found each other. But we believe in fate, Rebels, and we think our paths would have crossed somehow. If not at a book club, then in some other way. Some people are just meant to come

together. And meeting each other was like a home-coming we didn't know was waiting for us.

From that very first conversation, it was clear that we fit seamlessly into each other's lives, which is how you know someone is a good friend. They don't expect you to rearrange your whole world for them – they step in and everything's brighter for it. We consider each other to be our true blue for many reasons, but one of the great signs of trust and support in our friendship is that we also encourage each other to seek out other nurturing relationships.

Rebels, as you get older, you're going to find yourself setting foot in all sorts of places. It can be both terrifying and electrifying. Whether it's a new after-school activity or summer trip,, you're going to have many opportunities to meet new people. That doesn't mean the friends you've made before are going to be left behind. It's the opposite. It's just that as you grow, your circle will grow.

It's cause for celebration. When Sara goes home to Kansas City, she can pick up with her college friends like she never left. When Camila's childhood friends visit Charlotte, they go back to all the places they loved when they were younger. There is a place in our heart for everyone who's touched it, no matter where we met or where we go. But in the same vein, just know there's never a shortage of love inside us. It's renewable! It's free! It's the greatest joy on Earth to seek out new friendships wherever we go.

It's rare in life that we can have the best of both worlds, but with friendship, you can have the old and the new. You can make a new friend in your painting class and still see your bestie next door all the time. If you greet life with open arms, it might just give you what you're looking for.

Where to Find New Friends

Even though we know the world is a big place, it can feel small. That's why it's important to try things out of your comfort zone – not only because it'll help you grow, but because it's where you'll meet people. If you're scrambling to come up with ways to meet your next bestie, ask yourself what it is that gets you excited and follow that feeling.

* **If you catch yourself singing in the shower or fantasising about being on set on your favourite show** . . . then it may be time to tap into your creative side. Why not audition for the school play or see if your drama club needs an extra set of hands? You have so much imagination inside you that it'd be a shame not to share it with the world.

* **If you like friendly competition and you always feel your best after a work-out** . . . then you should try out for the football team or try your hand at tennis. It's basically a rule of life that teammates share a special bond. Working together out on the field is a great way to build friendships. Bonus tip: watch *Bend It Like Beckham* as a group and prepare to get emotional.

* **If you've always wanted to make a difference in your community** . . . then you might try volunteering at a nearby community garden, soup kitchen, or animal shelter. You have a big heart, and it won't be long before other people take notice.

* **If you think school is a breeze and are feeling up to an extra challenge** . . . then you should get involved with extracurricular activities, like debating, robotics club, or Model UN. Give that brain a work-out and meet others who love learning just as much as you do.

WHEN WORLDS COLLIDE

By the time I turned 25, I had lived in five different cities and switched jobs three times. Rebels, that is a lot of change in a short amount of time! But what I'm most thankful for is the people it brought into my life. I still talk to my then-work bestie even though we no longer live in the same city. I'm in a book club with my childhood best friend. When I'm in Los Angeles, I have my core group of friends, but I also love it when my other friends come to visit. If I'm feeling adrift, I can close my eyes and imagine a map in my head. I can pinpoint all of the places where there's someone I love.

But it wasn't always this way. When I was your age, I used to think you could have only one best friend forever. But life is much richer when you allow yourself to be open to new friends wherever you go. Even though Camila is my ride-or-die for all things book- and movie-related, I love getting dressed up with my friend Alyx and going to fancy dinners. Or when I know I need to buckle down and work, my friend Ashley is my go-to for a study date.

My point is this: we contain multitudes, so it makes sense that we find different people for our different needs and interests. And that's OK. You can love everyone equally but not in the same way. It's what makes life exciting, knowing that we will never love the same way twice, that we carry that abundance in us always.

As I've grown up and maintained these friendships (through FaceTime calls, vacations, and even a letter once in a while), all of my friends have got to know one another too. Nothing warms my heart more than getting everyone together

and introducing them to the other people I share my life with. We've said this before, but we *love* a bestie-in-law, otherwise known as a friend of your best friend.

Activities for a Group

When meeting your bestie-in-law or introducing two besties, you can be creative about your meet-up. Maybe your football-loving friend is staying with you for spring half-term, and you know your drama club co-star would adore her. Or maybe you just joined the robotics team, and you want to host a getting-to-know-you party. Either way, the more the merrier!

* **Potluck:** Why pick just one cuisine when you can have many? Gather your friends and invite them to a dinner where everyone brings a beloved dish. You can try a little bit of everything and still share your favourite meal with your friends. Nothing says cosy and intimate like a full belly and laughter at the dinner table.

* **Capture the Flag:** Work up a sweat with some friendly competition (key word: friendly!) with this classic outdoor game. Sharing a goal (in this case: winning) bonds people together super fast.

* **Karaoke:** Is there anything better than the feeling of singing along to your favourite song with your best friends? Stun your group with a well-practised solo or bring everyone together in shared harmony to hit those notes in *High School Musical's* "Gotta Go My Own Way."

The More the Merrier

One of the most valuable lessons we've taught one another is that love is a renewable resource (you're going to hear a lot about that in this book!). That is to say, love is most beautiful when it's allowed to be free. And you, Rebels, are full of love. There is never a shortage of love to give, and there is no limit to the love you can receive. That's why it's so silly to think we can have only one best friend. Some people do have one person they consider their bestie. And that's great! But others have several best friends. No matter what your best friend situation is, it can be nice to have multiple fulfilling relationships.

Here's a hard truth we both learned in our teens: sometimes we make the mistake of pouring too much into one cup. We know what happens when we do that – it overflows. And if we're not careful enough, it spills and the cup breaks.

Human beings are much more complicated than ceramics, but the same principle applies. We have so many different interests and needs that it's not fair to expect one person to fulfill all of that (or to be the person doing all that fulfilling). Not only is it OK to have multiple friends, but it's also *healthy*. It doesn't mean that you love one friend more than the other. It means you love them in different, deeply meaningful ways.

A best friend is just a title, but the people are not interchangeable. For example, we consider each other to be best friends on Earth (and even to the sun and moon and back), but we have other friends who mean just as much. And the better part? We're all friends with one another. Camila's childhood best friend, Gwen, and Sara like to refer to themselves as *besties-in-law*.

Together, the three of us create a wonderful ecosystem of laughter, kindness, and support. We know it may seem like having multiple best friends is the opposite of what we know about friendship, but we're telling you your world will be all the brighter for it.

    Let yourself blossom, Rebels. There's too much love to spread and receive to just be rooted in one place.

Getting to Know Your Friends Better

Rebels, we're constantly learning more about ourselves and our friends. It's not because we're not already close (we talk every day!), but because when you love someone, you never stop growing and learning and exploring. You'd be surprised what there is still to be learned about your best friend.

To take this quiz, write down your answers on separate pieces of paper. Read the questions out loud one at a time and, if you correctly guessed what your friend wrote on hers, then you get a point.

But remember: it's OK if you're still finding out new information about each other. This isn't about winning or losing or who loves who most.

1. What is the name of your childhood pet?
2. How did the two of you meet each other?
3. What is the comfort movie you watch when you're sad?
4. What is your dream job?
5. Who is a celebrity you're dying to meet?
6. What is something on your summer bucket list?
7. Out of all the meals in the world, which one is your favourite?
8. What is a secret talent of yours?
9. What is your greatest strength?
10. What is a place you've always wanted to visit?

A KALEIDOSCOPE OF COLOURS

WHAT THE REBELS SAY

"There is nothing I would not do for those who are really my friends. I have no notion of loving people by halves, it is not my nature."
—Jane Austen

One of the wonderful things about being a part of the Rebel Girls sisterhood is the reach of it. There are many differences that can exist within a person – like race and religion – but certain aspects of being a girl are universal.

Our similarities are like stepping stones into one another's hearts. But people aren't interchangeable. The differences within everyone are deep and wide. The hope is that we learn from one another's differences and that the knowledge we gain is respected and cherished. The hope is that we let it change us.

One of the first friends I ever had, Kim, is someone I'll always think fondly of. I remember us at six years old, sitting in

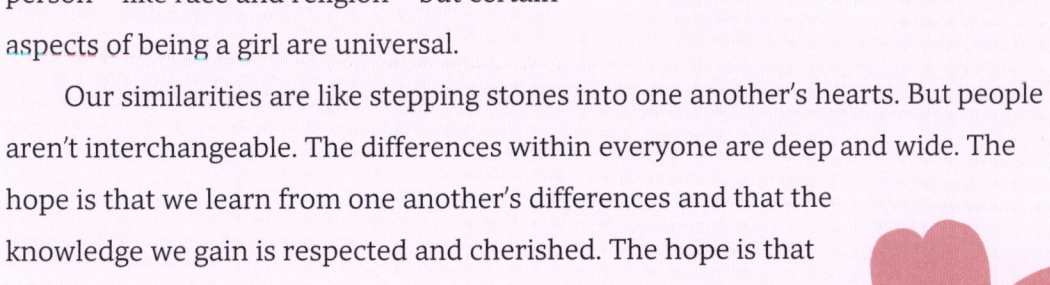

her spotless house, with our socks slipping against the hardwood. I remember her telling me about her family history and how her parents had to escape from their dangerous homeland to start over in the United States. I also remember being in awe of her family. I may not have understood the information entirely, but I realised it was important all the same. I was honoured by her trust in me then. I am honoured now.

Even though we haven't seen each other in some time, I still have a lot to be grateful to her for. Our friendship was the first I had ever experienced outside of my comfort zone. Before Kim, I was really only friends with the children of my parents' friends. With Kim, though, everything was brand new. I had never eaten Korean food before I met her. I had never cared about anime, but after watching the first few episodes with her, I also became obsessed with *Hamtaro* (way before your time, Rebels, but I still recommend it!).

It's always nice to connect with people who are similar to you. But it can be even more satisfying to connect with someone who's a little different, someone who can open your eyes to new things and who you can share your ideas with. And the truth is, no matter how long you know someone or how alike you think you are, your friends never stop surprising you. Discovering a difference in a friend you thought was your #twin is more than a wonderful surprise. It's a renewed opportunity to fall in love with your friend all over again.

WHAT THE REBELS SAY

"The thing to do, it seems to me, is to prepare yourself so you can be a rainbow in somebody else's cloud."
—Maya Angelou

THE EBBS AND FLOWS OF FRIENDSHIPS

> **WHAT THE REBELS SAY**
>
> "There is a natural ebb and flow to friendships. There are times you think there's nothing left between you, that you've hit the bottom, but the special ones survive, and find ways of restoring themselves."
> —Colette McBeth

Did you know our ears and noses will keep on growing and growing, long after the rest of our body is done? We almost never notice it, though! These parts of us grow at a snail's pace, bit by bit, so the change is almost imperceptible.

Friendships are like this too. When they're established, we sort of think, *"OK, cool. It'll be like this forever,"* mostly because we have no idea what the future will bring. All we ever have to go off of is the present moment, right? The thing is, we are changing with each new experience we undergo. It's only natural for our relationships to change as well.

It doesn't stop hurting when we realise things are different, though. Like when suddenly you and a friend are butting heads a bit more than usual, or when it seems like the girls at your lunch table have an inside joke you're not part of. The important thing to remember, Rebels, is that different is not always worse. Sometimes it's just . . . different. Even when it doesn't feel great, there's a lesson in everything. Still, what are we to do with these big feelings?

Why, accept them, of course! Life is long, Rebels. Personally, we have nurtured friendships for more than a decade, and in that time, we've grown closer to our friends, grown apart from them, moved thousands of miles away, moved back and basically lived in each other's pockets, moved away again, and on and on. Some of these friendships have grown stronger throughout it all. Some have simmered down and settled into a fond memory of "that time when we . . ."

C'est la vie (such is life). Like our hero, author Cheryl Strayed once said, "Acceptance is a small, quiet room." It's bittersweet. We think that, even in moments of great distance (both physical and emotional), the love we have for people remains. That's the painful bit, right? We have all of this love for the other person, and they're not around to receive it. Love, however, isn't currency. It just is – like a summer breeze or spring rain. We don't try to slow down the wind or stop the rain, we accept it as a natural part of life.

Picture This

Jen met Mady on the first day of swimming camp. She knew they were going to hit it off when she cracked a joke during the ice-breaker introductions and Mady laughed at the reference. Now they're attached at the hip.

The summer is filled with fun now that Jen has met her new friend. They ride their bikes together in town and play video games at sleepovers. Mady's mum even takes them to the midnight release of the latest superhero movie! From where Jen is standing, it seems like summer is going to last forever, and she can't imagine life without Mady.

But when summer ends, things change. The girls go to different schools, and Mady is busy during the school year. She's the vice president of her school's nature club, and she does things with her Girlguiding unit on the weekends. She tries her hardest to make sure she meets up with Jen when she can, but their friendship has cooled off significantly.

The following summer, they're both back at swimming camp. Mady is acting like everything is normal, but Jen is feeling a little hurt. If Mady cared, she would have made more of an effort to see Jen over the school year and not just at swimming camp when it was convenient for her, Jen thinks. After all, actions speak louder than words . . . right?

What should Jen do? End her friendship with Mady and move on, or trust her friend with her feelings and try to work it out?

Sometimes, when a question seems too large for us to possibly know the answer, we look to nature for some help. What we've learned is that the land, our oceans, even the sky is always changing. It seems like an inevitable part of life, no matter how much we wish it wasn't. We never step into the same river twice, right? The water is constantly flowing, just like we are constantly changing. As you get older, you'll realise that ebbs and flows in a relationship are natural.

Last year, Jen thought friendship meant seeing someone every day. She had grown up going to school with the same group of kids, so her closest friends were the people she saw all the time. After talking it through with Mady, Jen realised she was just feeling anxious because she'd never had a long distance bestie before. But Mady let Jen know how much she valued their friendship and it's not anything Jen did or didn't do, it's just that she has a packed schedule.

Once Jen accepted that her friendships don't have to look the same, she could enjoy her special relationship with Mady and value it all the same. The two girls hugged it out and promised to make a standing appointment at their favourite ice-cream shop once a month. They end up having the best summer ever, two years in a row!

So you see, Rebels, friendships often evolve. Even when they change on the surface, if the foundation is good, you'll always have a friend in your corner.

What Vibe Do You Bring to Your Friend Group?

1. **If you could be any animal, what would you choose?**

   A. A koala bear. You're cuddly and caring. Not to mention, you're always down for a nice nap.
   B. A dolphin. You're playful and energetic. Exploring the ocean seems like the right kind of adventure for a curious soul like you.
   C. An owl. You're wise and give excellent advice. Your friends know you have their best interests at heart.

2. **Your besties are trying to cement plans for Saturday afternoon, and everyone is throwing out ideas. What do you suggest?**

   A. Self-care day. You're thinking face masks, manicures, pedicures, hair braiding – the works.
   B. Sports day. You feel your best when you're active and part of a team.
   C. Volunteer day. You're passionate about giving back to the community, and you can think of no better way to spend an afternoon than cleaning up your local park with your best pals.

3. **What is your favourite film genre?**

   A. Romance. You love to be swept up in the moment and enjoy it when the main characters get their happily-ever-after. You love love!
   B. Adventure. Whether it's an epic fantasy or the latest action movie, you get a thrill out of anything that makes your heart race.
   C. Drama. Gripping scenes, tear-jerker moments – you live for the spectacle of it all.

4. **You notice a friend is having a bad day. How do you cheer them up?**

   A. By giving them a big hug. You can't change the events of the day, but you can let your bestie know that no matter how hard the road gets, you'll be by her side.
   B. By handing them a pillow to yell into. Sometimes you've just got to let it all out, and your bestie knows you are a safe person to let out her feelings with.
   C. By letting them vent. Talking about a bad day can be super helpful, and you're a great listener.

5. **Which new hobby would you and your friends like to try?**

   A. Arts and crafts club. Creating together would be a blast. Break out the beads for some friendship bracelets.
   B. A sports team. Trying a new sport can be a bit intimidating. Good thing you have your friends to lean on!
   C. Book club. You and your group will love discussing the plot and characters of your next read.

6. **If you could have any superpower, what would it be?**

   A. Omni-communication. You'd be able to speak any language and even communicate with animals.
   B. Flying. Being able to soar through the clouds sounds awesome. You could swoop in and save the day!
   C. Super-intelligence. Your friends often look to you as the leader and, with this superpower, you could solve any problem that comes up.

Answers

Mostly As: Sugar!

You're probably #1 on a couple of friends' lists of people to call when they need a pep talk. Sensitive and dreamy, you have a knack for understanding just how your friends feel.

Mostly Bs: Spice!

Your friend group likely admires your determination. When the gang falls into a rut, you're there to amp everyone up again! You enjoy being your friends' cheerleader and feel very protective of them.

Mostly Cs: Everything nice!

You give big main character energy and probably enjoy taking the lead, which is just fine by your besties, who trust your ability to curate a vibe and make the plans.

ASK THE EXPERTS

Camila and Beth have some great advice about handling tricky friendship situations.

> How do you make new friends without making your old friends jealous?
> —Elle P., 13, California, USA

I used to spend so much time fretting over this question, but I've realised the answer is quite simple: communicate, communicate, and communicate some more! It's a testament to the empowering connections I have in my life that I feel confident enough to address my friends directly. I'm always asking, "Can you feel my love?" I'm asking them, "Do you feel appreciated?" In my experience, jealousy usually arises from feelings of neglect, so make sure you're nourishing the relationships you have as much as the ones you're currently cultivating.

Camila Rivera
Author

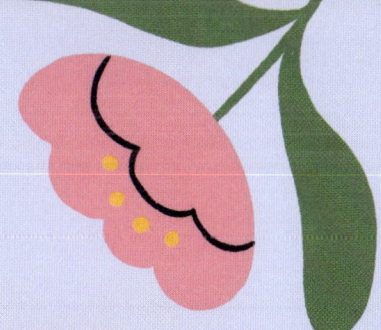

How do I navigate secondary-school cliques?
—Willa R., 11, New Mexico, USA

Navigating secondary-school cliques can be intimidating. I think it's a good idea to be an attentive observer and watch how different groups interact and treat others. If you keep in mind what qualities are important to you in a friend and look for kids and groups of kids who match those values, the chance is pretty high that you will find a group of people who will treat you with kindness and respect. If this ends up being something that you are struggling with, please go and see your school counsellor or another trusted adult so they can support you.

Beth Lucas
School Counsellor

CHAPTER 5
WHEN THE ROAD GETS ROCKY

The first time I ever cried because of a friend (a best friend, nonetheless!), I remember it hurt so bad that I could feel it in my chest. I'm not exaggerating. Sometimes heartbreak feels exactly like what it sounds like. I wish I could tell you that all your friendships will be smooth sailing. That they'll last forever, and no one will ever get their feelings hurt. But the reality is much messier, as you've probably discovered by now. The good news is, like a broken bone, heartbreaks will heal in time.

However much it stings at first, our hurts will fade. You've likely heard the phrase "What doesn't kill you will make you stronger," but I don't want you to be strong in the sense of being hardened and closed off. I want you to take what doesn't kill you and allow it to make you more empathetic, more understanding, and more sensitive to your own words and actions.

Sometimes our emotional wounds are lessons in disguise. As beautiful and exciting as this time period is, I also remember it as being devastating at times. And I want you to acknowledge that your feelings are valid, but also know that it will be OK in the end. Rebels, in this chapter, we're going to talk a lot about grace. Not just for other people, but for ourselves as well. Your friendships will hit some bumps in the road, but you'll learn how to ride them out and discover that often those bumps are worth it.

Even the best of friends miscommunicate and fight. It stinks (like, *really* stinks), but it's worth it for all the inside jokes and shared memories and support. Don't let momentary periods of pain eclipse all the joy that friendship has to offer.

CRACKING THE CLIQUE CODE

WHAT THE REBELS SAY

"The opposite of belonging is fitting in."
—Brené Brown

Let's talk about growing pains.

No, not the physical aches you sometimes feel in your legs. I'm talking about the heartaches you experience when something you've said goes unacknowledged or when your friend group "forgets" to invite you to a sleepover. It can feel like cliques are forming all around us, and sometimes we find ourselves on the outside of one. At one point in time or another, it happens to us all. Even me.

I've always been a drifter. I could fit into any clique comfortably, but I never really felt like I had a home. I never felt like I truly belonged anywhere. Maybe you've felt this way. You'd be surprised to know (though I'd bet anything it's true) that your peers likely feel the same way – even if they are lucky enough to belong to the "popular" clique.

Let me just take a moment to say this: cliques that exclude people or are unkind to others stink! Somehow, cliques have the power to make us question ourselves. Like, "Why don't they want me around? Is it my choice in fashion?

Is it the music I like (or don't like)?" Don't go down that rabbit hole, Rebels. A lot of the time, there is no rhyme or reason to why cliques exclude people. But I'll let you in on a secret. You might think insecurity is a marker of youth, but even adults exhaust themselves worrying about things like "Was I funny enough?" or "Did that sound weird?"

Cliques, unlike supportive, welcoming groups, have a way of making us doubt ourselves. When this happens, focus on your good qualities! It might seem like there's always someone who is funnier or cooler than you are. But that doesn't negate the fact that YOU are funny and cool too. (You *are* a Rebel Girl, after all).

Dealing with the Clique Effect

We spoke to an expert, Beth Lucas, about this very topic. Ms. Lucas has been a school counsellor at a secondary school for almost 25 years, so she knows how difficult dealing with cliques can be. Here are her top tips:

* **Recognizing that you are a part of a clique is the first step.** Be mindful of how this clique treats you and others. Is your clique kind, welcoming, and inclusive? If the answer is yes, keep up the good work! If the answer is no, take steps to make sure you are not contributing to a negative culture. You can do this by refraining from gossiping or treating people unkindly. If you are unable to help change the culture of your clique and it continues to hurt others, you may want to consider moving on.

* **If you are on the outside of a clique that is treating you unkindly, do your best to ignore what is being said and limit interactions with those people.** Try to spend time with people who have similar values and who treat you with kindness and respect. If the members of the clique continue to seek you out and treat you disrespectfully, tell a trusted adult who can help you.

* **Know that you do not have to be a part of a clique.** It is totally fine to have friends from different groups and not be committed to only one group. Having the ability to spend time with and interact with a variety of people is a skill you will use throughout your life. It gives you the opportunity to learn and experience all kinds of different things. Remember, you can never go wrong by welcoming others and treating them with kindness and respect.

SOS: ASKING FOR HELP

However (or wherever) it happens, bullying can be a devastating experience, whether it's you or someone you love who has to endure it. But that's the thing, you don't have to endure it! Pain may be an unavoidable facet of life, but we are firmly declaring this to you, here and now: YOU WERE NOT PUT ON THIS EARTH TO SUFFER. Suffering is a choice, and it often looks like the acceptance of unfair treatment.

Listen, Rebels. There is nothing that makes a person deserving of being bullied. So when you see someone being bullied – whether they are your friend, or not – your first thought should not be: *I wonder what they did to deserve it.* Your first thought should be: *How can I help them?* After all, if the roles were reversed, you'd want them to think the same for you.

Before you can help, though, you have to learn how to spot when someone needs help. Do you know what bullying looks like? Sometimes it's pretty obvious and involves things like rude comments and mean-spirited pranks, but other times it can be a little more difficult to spot. Let's go over some different forms of bullying.

WHAT THE REBELS SAY

"When my friend and I got into a fight recently, I explained my side and then listened to their side. We took a break, then talked it over more and moved on."
–Maggie P., 13, Idaho, USA

The Many Faces of Bullying

* **Cyberbullying:** Most cyberbullying happens on social media platforms like Instagram and TikTok. Cyberbullies will sometimes post mean comments on someone's photo or send hurtful DMs. Any bullying that takes place on digital devices – even gaming platforms! – can be defined as cyberbullying.

* **Verbal Bullying:** You might have heard this rhyme: "Sticks and stones may break my bones, but words will never hurt me." As you probably already know, that is so not true. Mean words can be just as harmful as physical bullying. Verbal threats can be scary, and name-calling can lower our self-esteem.

* **Social Bullying:** This type of bullying can be a little difficult to pin down, but you certainly know it when you feel it. For example, spreading nasty rumours, playing a mean prank, and excluding someone from social events are all signs of social bullying.

* **Physical Bullying**: Hitting, kicking, pinching – these are all familiar forms of physical bullying and are never OK. Physical bullying can also include purposefully ruining someone's clothes or stealing their stuff.

So, how do we deal with bullying? In order to fully answer that question, we'd have to get down to the root of why bullies exist. According to experts, bullies do what they do because they need attention and they're doing all the wrong things to get it. One of the most effective ways to combat a bully is to ignore them. Most bullies crave an audience, so even simple phrases such as "I'm not going to engage with this," and "Let's not do this," can shift the energy and quiet the bully.

Still, it's important that you don't feel like you have to do everything yourself. We know you're at a point in your life when independence is precious (rare as a diamond), so asking for help can feel like taking a step backwards. Let me be the one to reassure you: it's not. Even the most capable of adults need a shoulder to lean on sometimes. Learning to ask for help is just another one of those pesky growing pains, and it's nothing to be ashamed about.

If it's not the shame that's keeping you from reaching out to an adult about a bully, it might be fear. Sometimes we fear retaliation from bullies, and sometimes we fear that the adults in our life will be totally uncool about this.

Remember: you are not a powerless bystander, and you are never alone. You have a network of adults (whether your school teachers or your parents, grandparents, etc.) who are meant to protect you from harm, and that same network will listen to you. Together, you can come up with a way to handle the situation.

Who's Your Dial-a-Friend?

Here's an affirmation for you: *I am not alone in my struggles. There are people who care for me and support me because I matter to them.*

No matter how lonely growing up can feel, you are never by yourself. Whenever one of us feels overwhelmed, we schedule a FaceTime call to talk through our problems. Here's an activity for you: pull out your phone and star three contacts who would be great to call in a time of distress.

Here are some questions that can help you figure out who should be on your dial-a-friend list:

1. Who gives the best pep talks?
2. Who is calm in a crisis?
3. Who has the best advice?

FRIENDS DON'T HURT FRIENDS

Rebels, the worst advice I've ever been given, hands down, was if a crush was mean to you, it meant they liked you. Though I'm sure the person was trying to make me feel better, it just left me confused. Why do we express our interest through torment? And more importantly, why do we teach girls that it's OK? This book is obviously not about romance (though, arguably, friendships are the greatest form of love!), but the same sentiment applies. The advice that if someone teases you or is mean to you, that means they like you is not good advice. Friends shouldn't intentionally hurt friends.

I've talked a lot about good times with my friends in this book so far. But it's time to be real and share moments when I was not a good friend. I am not proud of this, but I hope by sharing my mistakes, I can help you side-step them. It's not fun to mess up, and it's hard to confess your mistakes, even years later.

Here's my secret: in secondary school, I was a bit of a bully. Not the push-you-down-on-the-playground-and-pull-your-pigtails type, but the mean girl variety. The type that made fun of people she didn't know and

stepped on others to make herself taller. There's nothing I can say to excuse that kind of behaviour, but I will say this: what many experts say about bullies is true. We do it because *we're* insecure and miserable. But out of all the people I hurt, the one that sticks with me most is Sidney.

Sidney and I were friends at secondary school from when we were 14 to 16. But the worse I felt about myself, the more I took it out on her. By the time we left school, we weren't on speaking terms. I used to tease her about things that I knew would hurt her. Ironically enough, I had learned that behaviour from my other friends, who also made fun of me in unkind ways. The circle of cruelty went around and around, and no one won.

You see, Rebels, it doesn't matter if you love someone if your actions are unkind. People remember the impact, good or bad. A good ribbing – a joke that everyone can laugh at, including the person it's directed at – is harmless here and there. But taunting, mocking, and outright tormenting? That's not friendship. That's a guaranteed way to end a friendship.

To her credit, Sidney never dished out what she received. She was always kind. Her refusal to let my actions influence how she treated others is one of the many reasons I admire her and why, years later, I emailed her a heart-felt apology.

Rebels, take it from me, if your friends are the ones making you feel bad about yourself, then they're not being good friends. They may change and grow, but it's not your job to reform them. Love is not supposed to hurt. You should always feel safe around the people you call your friends. They should be your cheerleaders, your confidants, and your compass.

Don't ever let yourself be convinced that friendship is something that needs to be suffered through.

Dial-a-Friend: Kristine Froseth

When I met my good friend Kristine Froseth (*Looking for Alaska*), we immediately bonded over one thing: we both struggle with having big feelings! Even though we live on opposite coasts, we still check in with each other frequently about our mental health. Kristine knows a thing or two about big emotions that may feel overwhelming, and here's what she wants you to know, Rebels.

When things get really tough, I use a self-care trick to calm down my heart rate. I start by filling up a bowl with ice and water, then I dunk my face in for about 45 seconds. It sounds a little nutty, but it works wonders for me!

If I don't have a bowl or ice around me, I try to ground myself with other techniques like box breathing (inhaling for four seconds, holding for four seconds, then exhaling for four seconds). I'll also try to write things out (I love a journal moment!) and reflect. Sometimes I'll text Sara a billion times when I feel like I'm spiralling – I am so lucky to have good friends I can lean on to help me cope.

Here's the bottom line: you are not alone. Our bad thoughts and emotions come and go like clouds. Honour your negative feelings and treat them like visitors coming through and then gently say, "Goodbye, it's time to leave now."

Digital Red Flags

You might be starting to think about getting a social media account. As exciting as the internet can be, it can be an unsafe place. It's important to take what you see online with a grain of salt. Sometimes the things we're insecure about IRL are magnified on places like Instagram, TikTok, or Snapchat. Here are some digital red flags to watch out for – and what to do about them.

* **FOMO:** Ugh. Who hasn't had a case of the classic fear of missing out? Social media makes everything worse, especially when you already feel like you're the only one being left out. Allow yourself to sit with your feelings, but remember that your worst thoughts aren't necessarily real. When I experience FOMO, I have to remind myself that I have hobbies and interests that I don't have to share on social media. What can you do today that'll bring you joy?

* **Me Versus the Better Me:** If you've ever had the thought that everyone else is prettier, smarter, more popular, richer, and more interesting than you online, you're not alone. And the good news? None of that is actually true either. The next time you're feeling down because of something online, journal what you love most about yourself. And reread that list the next time some app makes you feel like you're not enough.

* **Trolls are Trolling:** Bad faith users are like weeds – they pop up everywhere. But trolls feed off engagement, which is why the most effective way to end them is simply by not giving them your attention. The next time you encounter a stray troll online, use the block button and cut off their access to you. Your peace is precious and it should be protected at all costs.

HOW TO APOLOGISE

One of the most humbling lessons we learn in our lives is that we're not always right. Sometimes we lose our tempers, we misplace our blame, jump to conclusions - you name it. But just because we do something bad doesn't mean we're bad people. It just means it's time to make things right by apologising.

Apology Tips

Apologies take bravery. It can be tricky to find the right words! We asked school counsellor Beth Lucas for some tips on asking for forgiveness. Here are her top three:

1. First things first: Apologising is owning what you have done to hurt the other person. It requires that you hear what they have to say and acknowledge this, even if it is hard for you to see their perspective or if you did not mean to hurt them. We can only control what we say, not how it makes others feel!

2. The key to a proper apology is to let the person know how you are going to make it right. You have to show them through your actions that your words have meaning. You can do this by following through on what you said you would do to make it right, as well as by *not* doing what you did wrong *again*.

3. A meaningful apology might sound something like this: "I am very sorry I hurt your feelings. I was angry when I yelled at you, and I can see that my words were hurtful. I care about you and would never intentionally hurt your feelings. In the future, I will make sure my tone is respectful, and that if I am angry, I will walk away and wait until I am calm so I can speak to you appropriately. I hope you are able to forgive me."

It can be difficult to face the music and admit you've done something wrong. But thankfully, we're experts in this area. Even we, Camila and Sara, have totally got into tiffs! It doesn't mean we don't love each other. It just means that conflicts and misunderstandings are a natural part of life. Our love for each other goes beyond our mistakes, which is why we take the time to talk about our feelings and, when necessary, say we're sorry.

Picture This

Nicole comes back from vacation with her family and notices something's up with her friend group. Her pal Leah is sitting apart from their friends, looking dejected. Even weirder – no one mentioned Leah's absence at the lunch table. They just carried on as if everything was normal.

It takes Nicole a couple of days to pluck up the courage to ask her friends why the vibes are off. Apparently, Leah was responsible for spreading a mean rumour about another girl in their group. Nicole is shocked. That doesn't sound like something Leah would do.

Nicole resolves to talk to Leah about it. At Leah's house, the two have a heart-to-heart. Leah admits she's disappointed in Nicole. The two of them had always been close, so Leah was surprised when Nicole seemingly picked the group over her, especially when she had done nothing wrong.

Leah wasn't the one who spread the rumour. It was another girl who told Leah that she would make Leah's life miserable if she told anyone the truth. Nicole feels terrible. She apologises sincerely for not talking to her about this sooner.

At school the next day, Nicole invites Leah to sit at lunch with their friends again. She talks her friends into hearing Leah out, and pretty soon the whole thing is worked out! Apologies exchanged, hugs embraced, and now the group is even tighter than ever. Most importantly, they learned the importance of communication, especially when things get tough.

Are You Standing Up for Yourself?

1. **Someone keeps bringing up an embarrassing moment you had in class. It's not just teasing – it's flat out rude. How do you respond?**

    A. Ignore it and hope they'll stop.
    B. Laugh it off – you can't let them get to you.
    C. Say something like, "It's not nice to pick on people. Let's talk about something else."

2. **You heard a mean rumour about someone in your class. You don't know them well, but you know that you'd be devastated if it were you. Even worse, you know it was your friend who started it. What do you do?**

    A. Well, it doesn't involve you, so you just hope more people move on soon . . .
    B. Be extra nice to the classmate.
    C. Shut the rumour down when people talk about it and tell your friend that it's not cool to be mean.

3. **Lately, you get the feeling no one is listening to you at the lunch table. You're often spoken over, even when you do try to talk. What do you do?**

    A. Stay quiet and hope they'll remember you're there.
    B. Go sit somewhere else.
    C. Tell them, "Hey, guys, I have something to say too!"

4. **Your best friend betrayed you in a big way. They told a secret you shared with them in confidence and now the entire school knows. How do you react?**

    A. You make sure you never tell them a secret again.
    B. Give them the silent treatment.
    C. Have a discussion with them about what they did and how it's affecting you.

5. **You team up with your besties for a group project, but you find yourself doing most of the work. How do you handle this situation?**

    A. Do all the work yourself. It's just easier this way.

B. Confront them. If they were your real friends, this wouldn't even be an issue.
C. Involve an adult to mediate the situation so everyone feels heard. After all, you never know what may be going on at home.

6. **Your new friend suggests you dye each other's hair. You know your mum would be furious, but this friend is a little pushy... What's your next move?**

A. Let her dye your hair. It'll grow out eventually... right?
B. Call your mum and ask—on speakerphone. Your friend will listen to your mum if she won't listen to you.
C. Give a firm no. If you receive pushback, you remind your friend that "No" is a complete sentence.

Answers

Mostly As:

You like all your social interactions to be smooth sailing – don't we all! But sometimes, you do have to rock the boat. Not speaking your mind hurts you in the long run – how will things change if you don't ever acknowledge what's not working in the first place? Try and take small steps towards being the captain of your own life.

Mostly Bs:

You know what's right for you. Sometimes, though, you're unsure how to express yourself. Here's a tip: when something makes you feel uncomfortable, don't feel like you have to act on it right away. Take a beat to think about how best to handle it. And don't be afraid to get advice from your grown-up.

Mostly Cs:

No matter how difficult it can be, you know the value of speaking up. You know how to stick up for yourself while also giving other people an opportunity to apologise. Keep it up! And remember that sometimes it's OK to ask for help – you don't have to take everything on by yourself.

ASK THE EXPERTS

We all go through tough times. Here, Sara and Beth answer your questions about the sometimes bumpy road of friendship.

> What do I do if I have friends in different groups who don't get along?
> —Daphne W., 8, South Dakota, USA

Oh, Rebels, I've been there. It's *hard*. Sometimes people just don't connect with one another. But what is important is everyone *respecting* one another. That means: no bad mouthing, no bullying, no mean-spirited teasing, etc. Don't try to force your friends into getting along, but don't tolerate rudeness either. And make plans to spend time with each group separately. There's no reason you should miss out on spending time with people you like.

**Sara Jin Li
Author**

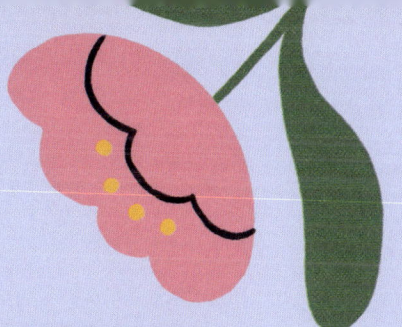

How do I help a friend who is being bullied?
—Evelyin J., 10, Florida, USA

You can stand up for a friend by being there with them and for them. You can encourage them and be a listening ear. Simply walking away from the bully with your friend and finding another place to be every time the bully says something mean or acts exclusionary might be enough – bullies thrive on attention. If that doesn't work and you feel safe speaking up, you can ask the bully to stop. If you don't feel safe, this is a time when you should ask for the help of a trusted adult.

Beth Lucas
School Counsellor

CHAPTER 6
MOURNING A FRIENDSHIP

Despite your best intentions, your friendship has come to an end. Ugh. I am so, so sorry, Rebels. Friendship break-ups can be really painful. The loneliest I've ever felt has been right after a break-up with a bestie.

Even though I knew it wasn't in our best interest to be friends anymore, I still missed the idea of her. I missed having someone who knew what I was thinking with just a look and who liked all the same music I did. I missed knowing there was always someone on the other side of the telephone.

I missed the specific things too. I missed her sense of humour and how she loved to dance. When you love someone, you'll miss them when they're gone. No matter how things went down, or who is responsible, it's totally OK to feel blue.

I give you permission to cry. Let yourself feel the full weight of your grief – all of the shame and disappointment and deep sadness – and make your peace with it. And remember: you might feel very sad right now. But you won't feel this way forever.

BEST FRIENDS ~~FOREVER~~

By now, we've got to know each other a lot, so here's a secret: we, Sara and Camila, are both cheesy, sentimental softies (we say with affection). And one thing that never fails to make us weep – just a little – is thinking back to all of our former friendships, even at our big-girl age. Even years later, we can tell you exactly what our last conversation was and why things ended the way they did. No matter how much older or wiser or more understanding we get, there will always be a little part of our hearts reserved for the friends who have come in and out of our lives.

The truth is, humans are all like fragile pieces of ceramics. Everyone has stories of good times and bad. In Japan, there is an art form called *kintsugi*. It is the method of repairing pottery with gold – rather than hiding the cracks, you can see exactly where it was broken and how it was put back together.

To survive a friend break-up, remember kintsugi. What did not work out made us stronger for what will. But the only way to overcome something hard is to go through it, so allow yourself to be sad, angry, confused, and lost.

In time, whether it be five weeks or months or sometimes even years from now (everyone heals at their own pace, Rebels!), you will appreciate your friendships, even the ones that didn't last. At this stage in your life, it's natural for some relationships to end. But even though it's part of growing up, it doesn't make it any less heart-breaking. Regardless of what led you and your friendships to their conclusions, know that it will make sense in time.

Common Types of Friend Break-ups

Distance: It finally happened to you: you met someone you just *clicked* with and, all of a sudden, one of you had to move. Maybe you tried to keep in touch, but things got busy and slowly communication faded. This has certainly happened to both of us and we were devastated. But remember:  the connection you shared will always be there. Nothing can take away from your bond and, in time, you'll be able to look back fondly at the memories and cherish what you had.

Growing Apart: This one might be the most common. One day, you were each other's soulmates and suddenly it seems like you're just not vibing. One of the bittersweet realities of growing up is that you will evolve and change. And certain people might not fit into your life in the same way any more. That's OK! You can always remember the happy times you shared.

Irreconcilable Differences: Ouch! This type of break-up usually involves a fight. When we say break-up, this is what we think of, and we won't mince words, Rebels – it's brutal. There's no worse feeling than losing a friend because of a disagreement. It can feel like someone's swept the rug out from under you.

Sometimes we try our best to make a friendship work, and it just doesn't. Even if it doesn't make sense at first, know that one day you'll look back and be thankful this break-up happened.

Broken Hearts Club Playlist

When you're going through a friend break-up, it's helpful to know you're not alone. Here are some songs to remind you that what you're going through isn't unusual and you'll get through it!

1. "Don't Speak" — No Doubt
2. "I Will Be" — Leona Lewis
3. "New Friends" — Jordana Bryant
4. "Tell Me How" — Paramore
5. "People You Know" — Selena Gomez
6. "High Horse" — Kacey Musgraves
7. "good 4 u" — Olivia Rodrigo
8. "Go Your Own Way" — Fleetwood Mac
9. "Don't Forget" — Demi Lovato
10. "Closure" — Taylor Swift

Picture This

Gia is the captain of her dance squad. She *loves* dancing, and she's been doing it since she was three. It's where she met her ex-best friend Allie. Their friendship ended after Allie lied about cheating on a test and accused Gia of cheating instead!

Ever since their friendship ended, dancing has made Gia feel a little sad sometimes. It reminds her of the fun they had together practising new moves or helping each other get ready for a recital.

After a while, though, Gia starts to feel passionate about dancing again. Rather than reminding her of Allie, it helps her move on from the pain.

Then, the unthinkable happens. Gia hears through the dancing grapevine that Allie's dance studio has suddenly closed down.

So many thoughts run through her head and – let's be honest – not all of them are kind. She tries to forget it's happening, but every few days, Gia finds herself thinking about it again.

If she was being honest with herself, Gia would admit she's a little pleased by the news. It feels a bit like karma. Gia is a little ashamed of herself – it's an ugly thought, after all – but it's also tenderly human. Here's the thing though: Gia isn't just a human, she's a Rebel Girl.

After a moment of soul-searching, she realises her reaction to the news meant that she expected Allie to be hurt by it. As if that made it OK that Gia was hurt too. (It definitely doesn't). Instead of allowing herself to settle in that hurt, Gia decides to stretch herself in the direction of goodness and bigness.

She reaches out to Allie and invites her to join her dance studio, and Allie is grateful to be dancing again.

In the story above, Gia realised that just because they aren't friends anymore doesn't mean they had to be enemies either. Maybe it would be uncomfortable at first, but they could share the same space. They could be civil. The goal should be to have mutual respect in the end, if nothing else. Obviously, it takes two to make this a reality. That means the dream won't always come true. But you know what? You'll never regret trying to achieve it.

Knowing When to Walk Away

Sometimes, a friendship is over long before goodbyes are said. It's more of a slow process – like a sweater with a snag that unravels over time. Everything that comes after that initial catch just seems sort of inevitable. Then there are times when it happens suddenly – one day you're clicking and everything's fine and the next, it is so not.

But how do you know when it's time to move on from a friendship? That's a tough question for a lot of people to answer.

We have to admit, we, Camila and Sara, can be overthinkers. As a rule of thumb, we give people the benefit of the doubt. We are always trying to see the other side of things. We don't make decisions lightly. We want to make the best (or the kindest or most forgiving) decision we can. But making the "best" decision can depend on a lot of things. Like, best for who?

At the end of the day, the answer to that question should be "me." Best for me! You have to look out for yourself as much as you do anyone else, Rebels. Consider your options and pay attention to how you react. The sidebar below will help you check in with your feelings.

Gut Check

Meditate or journal about each question for a moment (works best if it's in silence!). Think about a particular person and, as you go through the list, take note of how your body feels and any reactions or thoughts that may come up.

1. Does this person talk to you with care or with disrespect?
2. When you go to see them, do you feel excited or anxious?
3. Do they listen to you or always talk over you?
4. Do they gossip a lot – about you and/or anyone else?
5. How do you feel about yourself in their presence?
6. Do you feel comfortable around them or does it feel like you're walking on egg-shells?

Remember, trusting yourself is a big part of growing up. You're *not* over-reacting. If just hearing someone's name makes your stomach drop, then maybe it's time to re-evaluate what their role in your life looks like. You deserve to be picky about who you share your time with.

HOW TO SURVIVE A FRIEND BREAK-UP

Allow me to indulge in my theatrical ways for a minute and say that there has never been a friendship break-up that hasn't wrecked me. In my opinion, friendship break-ups aren't talked about enough. I used to wonder why that is – I guess it's because we don't expect our friendships to come to an end. After all, there's a reason why we say best friends *forever*.

I've had one friendship end because of distance and another end because of a fight. I remember the pain of those friendship break-ups well, but I also remember the things I did to heal.

On the next pages, we'll walk through some steps you can take to move forward after a friendship ends. Things like joining a new club, spending time on your favourite hobby, and journalling about your feelings will all help the hurt subside.

When you move on in a healthy way, time will naturally heal the wound. And remember: you're not alone. Friendship break-ups are a rite of passage. As people leave your life, they make space for new friends to

come along. Sometimes they leave things tidy and soft, sometimes they make a big mess on their way out. But love is a renewable resource (remember?) and as sure as I am that the sun will rise tomorrow and the next day, I know friendship will come back to you too in another form.

Dial-a-Friend: Kyndra Sanchez

You might know Kyndra Sanchez as Dawn on *The Baby-Sitters Club*. On and off set, Kyndra knows how important friendships are – and how difficult it is when one ends. Here, she shares some great tips for getting through a friend break-up.

To all the young girls going through a friend break-up, here's some heart-felt advice: first, it's absolutely OK to feel a whirlwind of emotions. Talk to a family member or another friend about what you're experiencing. Sharing your feelings can be a big relief. Next, give yourself time to heal. Engage in activities you enjoy, like reading, drawing, dancing, or playing a sport. These passions can help mend your heart. Lastly, don't rush into finding a new friend. Genuine friendships develop naturally over time. Be open to meeting new people, but let it happen organically. Remember, you're incredible just as you are. Your worth isn't determined by anyone else. Focus on self-love and self-care. Friend break-ups can be painful, but they teach us valuable lessons about resilience and self-worth. You're strong, and you'll emerge from this experience even stronger. Keep your chin up, and don't forget how amazing you are!

A Five-Step Plan to Getting Over a Friend Break-up

There's no perfect remedy for a broken heart, but these ideas can help you feel a little bit better.

* **Throw a Pity Party:** Listen . . . sometimes wallowing is necessary. Take a few days to snuggle up in your softest pyjamas, eat your favourite comfort foods, and cry it out. Research says crying is our body's way of releasing pain. Let yourself mope and be gentle with yourself.

* **Get Some Distance:** As tempting as it is to see what your former friend is up to by going to their social media pages or heading to your old meet-up spot, it's not the best idea. Sometimes it's unavoidable that you'll share space with them, but if you're able to give each other some distance, that's often the best move.

* **Self-Care Weekend:** What would you do to cheer up a friend who's feeling bad? Then treat yourself to those very same things. Whether it's a manicure or maybe a trip to the shops, just focus on what will make you feel just a little bit better again. Don't forget to stay hydrated and get lots of sleep!

* **Write Your Former Friend a Letter:** But don't send it. When we're left with a lot of emotions, it's important to find an outlet for them. Write everything you're feeling and seal it in an envelope, but never, ever give it to them. This is a release. This is just for you. You'll feel a lot better with everything off your chest.

* **Clean Your Space:** Rebels, think of this as your ritual. Our environment really affects us, so it may be a good time to take inventory of what's around you. Pictures of the two of you? Time to take them down. The jacket they left and the books they lent you? Give them back. You need to make way for the new, after all.

* **Distract Yourself:** Without your former friend in your life, you might have some extra time on your hands. Fill it with some positive, joyful activities. If you've been interested in learning to cook, see if there's a class you can sign up for. If you're an animal lover, maybe there's a pet shelter where you can volunteer. Having exciting things on your calendar will make moving on much easier.

THE OTHER SIDE OF THE RAINBOW

You. Have. Done. It!

After all those sad playlists, and all those car rides home staring out of the window dramatically, you are on the other side of the friendship break-up. Sure, it still hurts sometimes. Maybe you haven't been able to bring yourself to throw out the friendship bracelet just yet, or maybe you still can't quite stomach seeing your ex-bestie's profile online, but you're starting to see the light at the end of the tunnel. You're being reminded less and less of your old friend as time goes on. You're even thinking about joining something new, like the chess club or your local football league. Maybe you're even thinking of inviting the nice girl who sits next to you in maths class over for a movie night.

Remember to celebrate these small wins. I know it feels like there isn't much to celebrate right now but, if nothing else, there is this: you survived it. You are resilient. You are a role model to broken hearts everywhere.

Am I giving off cheerleader vibes? I hope so! It's one of the traits I'm most proud of – being my friends' biggest cheerleader. And after all this, I feel like I'm already one of yours. So here I am, your own personal cheerleader!

Over the years, I've learned that an unfortunate side effect of sadness is the tendency to turn into a Negative Nancy. It's what happens when you spend so much time after a break-up going over what (possibly) went wrong.

Don't dwell on the negative. Your energy would be much better spent focusing on the sweetness, rather than the bitterness, of a bittersweet situation. And, Rebel – life is full of them. So lean into the sweetness. Cherish the good times you've had, even if the people you had them with are no longer around. Savour the constant and steady friendships you still have.

And take the time to be sweet to yourself. Not sure how? Here, I'll start.

For all these reasons, you will make amazing friendships again.

Phew . . . listen. I know it's a tall order. Getting over the end of any friendship is a struggle. Now I'm asking you to open yourself up, *again*? After last time?? Even after you barely survived???

You're resilient. You're more than just a girl – you're a Rebel Girl. I believe in you. You *can* heal from the past. You *can* trust yourself again. It's not enough for me to believe in you, though. You have to believe in yourself. More than that, you have to believe in endings as something more than just endings. They can be beginnings too.

Whoa, what a realisation! The idea that not everything is black and white and that many things can be true at once took me a few years to learn. More often than not, everything is happening simultaneously. A door may close but a window opens. You may lose a friend but end up finding yourself.

At the end of the day, the sum of who we are can only really be measured by what we choose to do in a crisis.

Here's a quote we love from writer Cheryl Strayed: "You will learn a lot about yourself if you stretch in the direction of goodness, of bigness, of kindness, of forgiveness, of emotional bravery. Be a warrior for love."

So, in your darkest moments, I want you to stretch towards the light. I want you to reach for your highest self. I want you to become the person you were always meant to be: a warrior for love.

WHAT THE REBELS SAY

"We should never want to become anyone else, because the greatest fulfillment we can ever get out of life is by becoming the best possible version of ourselves."
—Alexi Pappas

How Should You Mend Your Hurting Heart?

1. **If you could have a heart-to-heart with anyone, who would it be?**
   A. Selena Gomez
   B. Michelle Obama
   C. Judy Blume
   D. Meghan Markle

2. **What colour speaks to you?**
   A. Lilac
   B. Burnt orange
   C. Maroon
   D. Forest green

3. **Who is your favourite heroine?**
   A. Princess Jasmine from *Aladdin*
   B. Hermione Granger from the Harry Potter series
   C. Katniss Everdeen from *The Hunger Games*
   D. Annabeth Chase from the Percy Jackson series

4. **What quote are you saving to your phone?**
   A. "True beauty in a woman is reflected in her soul. It is the caring that she lovingly gives, the passion that she knows." —Audrey Hepburn
   B. "You're more trouble than you're worth." / "I'm a girl. That's my job." —Tamora Pierce, *Street Magic*
   C. "Take your broken heart, make it into art." —Carrie Fisher
   D. "The way I see it, if you want the rainbow, you gotta put up with the rain." —Dolly Parton

5. **Where do you prefer to spend alone time?**
   A. A library
   B. A movie theatre
   C. Outdoors
   D. The kitchen

6. **Who was the last person you texted?**
   A. Your parents
   B. A sibling
   C. A classmate
   D. Your crush

Answers

Mostly As: Call a Loved One

We all need a friendly ear once in a while – and that's exactly what the people who love you want to give you. Reach out to someone you respect and who knows you well, like a parent, aunt, uncle, or teacher. There is a 100 per cent chance that they've lost a friend in their life too and will have some wisdom to offer you.

Mostly Bs: Movie Marathon

Sometimes we just need to immerse ourselves in someone else's world. Curate the ultimate movie marathon and treat yourself to some popcorn and chocolate. Watching our favourite films can be cathartic and a necessary reminder that sadness, while temporary, is part of being alive. Load up your Netflix queue and settle in for the night.

Mostly Cs: Journal

Take it from your friendship elders: the only way out is through. What we mean by that is you have to give yourself the grace to feel what you're feeling. We all cry, Rebels! Open up a notebook and jot down everything you're experiencing. You'd be surprised at how healing journalling is.

Mostly Ds: Sweat It Out

Scientists say that exercise is good for the mind, and they're right. As tempting as it may be to curl into yourself, it can be beneficial to get your heart pumping. Whether it's following along to a yoga video or playing a game of football with your neighbours, moving around will make you feel better. (Bonus: You can treat yourself to some ice-cream after!)

ASK THE EXPERTS

Check out Alexandra's and Beth's advice for setting boundaries and coping with feeling left out below.

> How do you deal with people who don't include you? How do you have confidence to put yourself in vulnerable positions?
> —Claire P., 13, Minnesota, USA

Being vulnerable is hard for everyone, even adults. Reminding yourself of all your positive qualities is very important. Positive self-talk is an easy way to do this. If you put in the time to think positively and reflect on the good things you have to offer, dealing with being excluded will be easier. That is not to say that being excluded is easy because it is hard. But keep trying. There are tons of activities and clubs where you can find kind friends with similar interests. Maybe you'd like to try a new sport or get involved with a Girlguiding unit? Trying new things helps us build confidence!

**Beth Lucas
School Counsellor**

> How can I say no to doing something I know I don't want to do or shouldn't do without people teasing me about it?
> —Stella G., 13, California, USA

Setting boundaries can feel kind of uncomfortable at first but once you are able to, you will feel much better about it. Boundaries help healthy friendships to last longer. Saying no to plans can be tough because you don't want to make your friends feel like you don't want to spend time with them, but typically a good friend will be understanding. The first step to communicating that you don't want to engage in certain plans is by responding in a timely manner. Don't put off responding. Take a deep breath and let your friends know you won't be able to make it this time. You can express to your friends that right now maybe you don't have the energy because you had a busy week or you are uncomfortable with the specific plans. You could also suggest shifting the meet-up to another day or come up with an alternative idea for plans that you feel more comfortable with.

**Alexandra Vaccaro
Psychotherapist**

CHAPTER 7
CELEBRATING FRIENDSHIP

Sara: Well, Camila. We did it!

Camila: Phew!

Sara: Ha! I won't lie to you, I did get a little misty-eyed writing this.

Camila: I'm proud of you for admitting it, my sweet, stoic, little earth sign. You already know I got misty-eyed writing this too. You wanna hear something interesting?

Sara: What?

Camila: When we sat down to write this book, I thought I knew exactly what I was going to say. In reality, every chapter challenged me to dig deep about the things I believed to be true.

Sara: I feel the same way. We wrote so much about our personal experiences with friendship (the good, the great, and the sad), and it was emotional getting to truly reflect on how we got here. Sometimes I'd read what you were writing and just go, "*Wow.*" Proof that we never stop growing, no matter how old we get.

Camila: Every day, I look at you and go, "Wow."

Sara: Please. Avert thy eyes.

Camila: [Laughs.] No, but seriously, writing this book with you was an amazing experience. I could think of no better ode to friendship. Aside from singing each other's praises, we left little breadcrumbs of our other friends all over the book.

Sara: We sure did. And what a great way to test if they really read this book. Kidding. Kind of.

Camila: LOL!

Sara: But on a serious note, I do hope we left some good take-aways for the Rebels here. Friendship is so important, and I want people's lives to be richer for it. Oh no, I'm getting emotional again . . .

Camila: Awww, bestie. I think they will be. This book came from the heart. Besides, it's our first step into the Bestie Hall of Fame. There's Taylor and Selena . . . there's Beyoncé and Kelly . . . Maybe one day, they'll say, "There's Camila and Sara!"

Sara: And you know what, that day might be today. But as usual, you're right. I don't know what else I can say other than I wouldn't have wanted to write this with anyone else but you, my true blue.

THE POWER OF FRIENDSHIP

Friendship is one of the best things in the world. When we, Camila and Sara, envision our future, it's always with each other and all of our other friends. It's not about how much money we'll make or where we'll be living (though anywhere on the beach sounds great), but the impact that we leave behind. A lot of things will come and go, but our friendships are our bedrock.

At this very moment, there's nothing that sounds more special than experiencing all our firsts with our friends: our first crush and our first heartbreak, our first sleepover, our first dance. Our tables will be full with laughter, warmth, and care. We'll all keep each other well-fed.

You've probably realised this by now, but our friends are our found family. And we know we're not the only ones. There's a long documented history of female friendships around the world, and we want to give some applause to just a few of them. And you never know – it could be you and your bestie on this list next!

Sarah Michelle Gellar and Selma Blair
From co-stars to besties: Sarah Michelle and Selma meet on set and become lifelong friends. These two have been part of each other's lives through successes, failures, birthdays, babies, and even Selma's experience with multiple sclerosis – a disease that affects the brain and the body. For 25 years (and counting), they have known each other, supported each other, and been present for the good times and the bad. What a gem it is to meet someone who loves you that much, and how special that they found each other by being lucky enough to get the same job.

Oprah Winfrey and Gayle King

It's hard to live in the US without having heard of Oprah and, by extension, Gayle – they are one of the most iconic friendship duos of our time. Nearly 50 years ago, the two met as young journalists in their early 20s and became friends after Oprah invited Gayle for a sleepover (because there was a snowstorm and Gayle couldn't get home). An everlasting friendship was born. Here's a little secret: keeping a friend for that long? It takes a lot of work. But it's amazing to know there is someone in the world who knows you as well as you know yourself, if not better. And if your friendship is what thousands of people want for themselves? It's probably a really, really good one.

Taylor Swift and Abigail Anderson Berard

When people talk about BFFs, it's hard not to think of Taylor and Abigail. The two met in their freshman year of high school (which Taylor wrote about in her song, "Fifteen") and, even though life took them in different directions, they remain a huge part of each other's lives. Finding someone as a teenager and getting to count on them through thick and thin, no matter what happens or how different your lives become? That's the dream!

Drew Barrymore and Cameron Diaz

Hands down, these two are bestie goals. They've had each other's back for more than 30 years, celebrating each other's success (like starring in the cultural phenomenon *Charlie's Angels* movies) and bearing witness to each other's failures. Cameron remained a steadfast friend, even when Drew was at her worst, because she believed in her bestie. It seems Drew never forgot that support, saying of Cameron that she is "one of the greatest friends anyone can ever have. She has so much love to give." It's heartening to know there are true-blue friends out there.

Looking Towards the Future

Did you know day-dreaming has positive health benefits? Not only has it been shown to reduce stress and anxiety, but it can help enhance creativity and problem-solving too!

One creative way to imagine your future is to create a vision board filled with photos, quotes, and illustrations that reflect your hopes and dreams. It's also a sweet way to bond with friends. Personally, our friend group really appreciates a crafty moment. One of the things that joins us together is our love for the arts! We use it as a way to understand ourselves – and each other – more deeply. We also use it to celebrate each other and, in doing so, celebrate ourselves.

What we mean is, we feel lucky to have a group of friends to trust our dreams with. Indulging each other feels like we're getting away with something delicious – like a sweet treat before dinner. Sometimes, we're dreaming of Italian villas and summers spent eating fruit and

listening to nothing but the wildlife. Mostly, we're just trying to imagine a bright future for each other, with each other in it. Give it a whirl! To start, here are some ideas for potential vision boards:

* **Artistic vision board**: If you don't know where to start, an artistic vision board is a good place. There's no theme to follow, unless you choose one. The theme is this: whatever you like. Fill your board with patterns, photographs, inspirational quotes – anything that speaks to you. This would be a good vision board to craft when you're feeling stressed.

* **Travel vision board**: This is a favourite among the besties. We love to brainstorm potential vacation spots. One of the few things we've agreed upon – and thus, set in stone – is a trip to Disney, in Orlando, Florida. We're thinking Epcot and taste-testing around the world. Maybe you and your besties can make a vision board of all the parks or other places you want to visit together.

* **Future career vision board**: You don't have to have your career goals all figured out right now. Still, it's nice to consider your options. Don't take this activity too seriously. In fact, the more out-of-the-box, the better. You never know, you might discover a hobby or career path you're truly passionate about.

* **Friendship vision board**: This vision board would make a heart-felt gift. A potential theme could be "How I see our friendship." You could fill this vision board with images that remind you of your bestie. Alternatively, you and your friends could each create vision boards based on what you think friendship is and compare the results. Who knows what you might find.

BEING PART OF THE REBEL GIRLS SISTERHOOD

As much as this book is an ode to friendship, it is also an ode to Rebel Girls everywhere. That means you! If nothing else, we hope that – in reading this book – you feel how special it is to be a part of this community.

You might not always be aware of it, but now, odds are there will always be a Rebel Girl nearby, waiting to lend a hand. That's what it means to be in community with others – it means to offer support to others, *especially* other girls. How do you know a Rebel Girl when you see one? That's tough! There are millions of us. Yet, despite our differences, we are alike in many ways that count. So the next time you spot someone who seems like a Rebel Girl like you, reach out. And, once you do, I promise you'll be surprised at the response.

We think being part of this sisterhood should be celebrated. And we have some ideas for how to do that.

Write a Letter to a Future Bestie: It's a little cheesy to say that you've yet to meet all the people you're going to love, but it's true. Right now, you're one day closer to finding another person that's going to illuminate your world and change your life for the better.

To look ahead, we suggest writing a letter to your future best friend. Grab a piece of nice stationery and your best pen. And when you meet your future true blue – and you will! – you can even give it to them. What a wonderful way to say that you've held space in your heart for someone: *Dear Best Friend* . . .

Throw a Party: Celebrating your friends is a great way to show how much you care. Maybe you'd like to throw your bestie a surprise birthday party. Or perhaps you'd like to plan a friendship anniversay party. Do you remember the day you met your dear friend? Even if you don't know the exact date, you can work together to pick a day and honour it every year. And remember that a party is what you make it. You don't need to buy cute branded cups or decorative treats from a trendy bakery. A party can be two pals and a carton of juice.

Start a Rebel Girls Book Club: In the spirit of being a Rebel Girl, starting a book club is the perfect way to not only celebrate your friendship, but to celebrate Rebel Girls through time. I mean, Louisa May Alcott? Rebel Girl. Mary Shelley? HUGE Rebel Girl! A book club is stimulating and educational, while being just plain fun. Talk to a grown-up about safe ways to reach out to the girls in your community, though a good place to start might be the bulletin board at school or your local youth club.

Picture This

On the playground, Mallory and Nina were sharing their feelings about the girls in their school. It seemed like their class was divided by cliques, and the girls wished everyone would get along better. They hatched a plan to start an after-school club and try to convince the other girls to join . . . but what should the club be about?

Nina suggests beading. Mallory was a whiz at crafting necklaces and bracelets, and the one time Nina wore one that Mallory made her for her birthday, she had received compliments from everyone.

Ater getting their club cleared by the school and finding a teacher to sponsor them, the girls post flyers they spent hours making the weekend before. They had decided to make it collage-style, hoping the nostalgic vibe would interest the trendy girls. Mission totally accomplished! When Mallory and Nina showed up to the club that afternoon, they saw three new girls waiting to join.

It was a slow start, at first. It was just the five of them cracking jokes and crafting necklaces after school. They'd talk about their interests (the latest show they watched, who their celebrity crush was at the time), but they also talked about selling the necklaces for charity. If they were raising money, what cause would they pick? They decide on a charity that helps mistreated animals, agreeing to donate the money they earned from the necklaces to a local animal shelter.

Word got out about what the girls were doing. Nina showed up and said her cousin in another school in the area heard about it and wanted to start her own chapter. Mallory and Nina were excited. Of course, they agreed. Pretty soon, girls all over the city were crafting necklaces for their cause. They decided to take their club online because it was getting too big to meet in person. One of the members ended up sharing a necklace on social media, and it blew up. Pretty soon, girls from all over the COUNTRY were participating!

Dial-a-Friend: Jordyn Curet

US singer and actor Jordyn Curet has some great advice for maintaining and celebrating friends even when you all have busy lives.

You can celebrate your friends by attending events they're participating in, such as sporting events, theatre performances, musical showcases, and more. This can make your friends feel special and show that you care about their interests. Also, be sure to check in with your friends every once in a while. Sometimes people get overwhelmed by their schedules, so checking in on your friends can mean a lot to them. You can invite them to do something together, such as watching a movie or going for a walk. It's these small acts of kindness that can make your friend feel supported and celebrated.

Ways You and Your Friends Can Give Back to the Community

A great way to bond with your friends is to do something meaningful for your community. Here are some ways to do just that:

* **Research and learn:** Start by looking into organisations and non-profits to get a feel for their missions. Learn about issues that are interesting to you, like endangered animals, climate change, or literacy. Pick the cause you feel most excited about.

* **Start small:** Does the butterfly effect sound familiar? The saying goes, "A butterfly flaps its wings and creates a breeze that can be felt on the other side of the world." It's about how tiny changes can be powerful. Look around your community. Would it benefit from a neighbourhood clean-up? Is an elderly neighbour in need of some help with their gardening? Is there a younger kid you know who could use some tutoring? Take on a few small acts of kindness together.

* **Reach out to an organisation:** Sometimes, the most precious thing we have to offer is our time. Do you and your bestie love spending time with animals? See if there's a shelter that needs an extra pair of hands. Are you both great at entertaining little kids? Maybe the youth club down the street could use your help.

IN CLOSING, REMEMBER TO...

* **Be supportive**: Above all else, we are here for each other. Whether you're helping a bestie through a hard time or being her biggest cheerleader as she accomplishes her dreams, be someone your friends can count on.

* **Be brave**: Rebel Girls don't hold back! Life is a wave, and we're here to surf it. Sure, things can get scary, but we meet each challenge with grace. More than that, we don't shy away from having hard conversations. The high road is a hard path to walk and not for the faint of heart.

* **Be honest**: We believe in integrity. Be honest with yourself and with your friends. Everyone in your life will appreciate that they can trust you.

* **Be loving**: Sometimes it's the easiest thing in the world. Other times it is an active choice you'll need to make. Either way, be patient and understanding with your friends and family, and show them what a big heart you have.

So go forth, Rebels! Spread positivity wherever you go. We know your lives will be filled with deep and meaningful friendships.

WHAT THE REBELS SAY

"I made six brand-new friends from dance competitions. It's lots of fun! We can talk about different things and cheer each other on because we are all dancers and love performing."
-Raffy, 13, Connecticut, USA

Friendships Around the World

Let's take a trip around the globe and observe how others celebrate friendship. Don't worry if you don't know the answers – this quiz is meant for you to learn some fun new facts to share with your friends.

1. **Which country does a White Elephant (or Secret Santa) gift exchange in September?**
   A. Colombia
   B. India
   C. Egypt

2. **In which country are anonymous love letters sent to close friends and family around Easter?**
   A. Italy
   B. Brazil
   C. Denmark

3. **Which country has buddy benches in schools, where students can sit if they're looking for someone to play with?**
   A. United States
   B. Canada
   C. Germany

4. **Which country celebrates Friendship Day on February 14?**
   A. Estonia
   B. Finland
   C. Ecuador

5. **Gift giving is the primary love language of which country?**
   A. Brazil
   B. South Africa
   C. Japan

6. **Which of these countries celebrate International Women's Day?**
   A. Italy
   B. Romania
   C. Chile

Answers

1. The correct answer is A, Colombia. The third Saturday in September is known as Dia de Amor y Amistad – the Day of Love and Friendship. Those with significant others will treat the day as Valentine's Day, and those without celebrate anyway! Usually, they'll organise a get-together with a group of friends.

2. If you guessed Denmark, you are correct. Also called *gækkebrev*, these cards are called snowdrop letters for the customary tradition of inserting a flower into each card.

3. All of them. A year 2 pupil named Christian Buck popularised buddy benches in the United States when he and his family were looking into schools in Germany, where they were thinking of moving. Since then, the idea has spread like wildfire across the world.

4. If you guessed A and B, you are correct. While the rest of the world is sending flowers and hearts to their love interests, the citizens of Finland and Estonia are sending one another heart-felt cards of appreciation. In fact, the Finnish national post service hires an extra 150 workers every year in preparation for the season.

5. While we're sure all of these countries have wonderful gift-giving traditions, Japan, in particular, places a strong emphasis on gifts. Exchanges are made during customary festivities (such as birthdays, weddings, and anniversaries), but there are also seasons specific to gift giving: Ochugen (1st July to the 15th) and Oseibo (from late November until 20th December).

6. All of these countries celebrate International Women's Day. In Italy, women and girls are given mimosa flowers to commemorate the day. In Romania, the day is treated almost like Mother's Day: men take the opportunity to recognise mothers, grandmothers, and friends with children, much as we do in the US. Chile takes a more revolutionary approach in celebrating IWD. The day is marked with demonstrations and marches, with protestors wearing green handkerchiefs as a symbol of support for women's rights.

ASK THE EXPERTS

Alexandra and Sara have some great advice for supporting old friends and making new ones.

My friend is shy in big groups. How can I help her feel more confident?
—Vivian G., 12, London, England

There are many great ways you can help your friend feel more comfortable and confident when in big groups. You can help build her confidence by practising some social behaviours with her such as maintaining eye contact, starting a conversation, and being mindful of her body language. Lastly, the absolute best thing you can do is to remind her how many awesome ideas and stories she has to share. All she has to do is be herself!

**Alexandra Vaccaro
Psychotherapist**

> What are your favourite ways to make new friends?
> —Avital Faye K., 11, Wisconsin, USA

I find it easiest to make friends by signing up for things I'm interested in. Like theatre. I met my BFF Malia in an acting class, and it was an instant bond because we were doing something we both loved. I would lean into what you genuinely love. Your passion for that will show and attract new friends to you. Plus, you'll be doing something that you enjoy too.

Sara Jin Li
Author

RESOURCES

Books

BFF or NRF (Not Really Friends): A Girl's Guide to Happy Friendships by Jessica Speer

Friendships are not always easy, especially as we get older. Thankfully, *BFF or NRF* is here to help our social relationships be as healthy as they can be. Find fun new activities to do with friends, learn how to handle bullies, and get tips on what to do when you hear gossip.

Real Friends by Shannon Hale

If you're a graphic novel fan, pick up this funny and sweet fictional book about two friends navigating secondary-school social dynamics, while trying to stay BFFs.

The Teen Girl's Survival Guide: Ten Tips for Making Friends, Avoiding Drama, and Coping with Social Stress by Lucie Hemmen, PhD

This book guides readers through the ebbs and flows of friendships. Plus, older girls who have been there offer their best advice for building a healthy social life.

Podcasts

The Girly Girl Podcast

Check out this life advice podcast from a fellow teen. Carmen Applegate provides helpful insights, answers questions, and shares stories from her own adolescence.

This Teenage Life

This conversational podcast connects young people around the world with each other as well as the adults in their lives to discuss the issues they are facing with sensitivity and care.

Pants on Fire

Looking for a podcast to binge with your bestie? This one is a lot of fun. In each episode, a kid interviews two experts on a particular subject – but one of them is lying! Can you figure out who?

Websites

Girls' Life | girlslife.com

A magazine and website centred around advice and entertainment guaranteed to guide you through your youth.

Your Life Your Voice | yourlifeyourvoice.org

Your Life Your Voice provides free trained counsellors to help you navigate whatever issues you may be going through, from depression and anxiety to bullying and coping with stress, and much more.

Miss O and Friends | missoandfriends.com

By girls, for girls, Miss O and Friends is a safe and supportive online community for teens and tweens. Log on to find life advice, fashion tips, and fun DIY ideas.

152

MEET THE AUTHORS

SARA JIN LI is an essayist, playwright, and filmmaker based in sunny Los Angeles, California. Her writing has been published in *New York Magazine*, *Elle*, *Cosmopolitan*, *Paper Magazine*, and more. As an immigrant and a queer woman of colour, Sara's artistic work centres marginalised identities. She has written several short films and plays, including *Leap of Love* – a satire about ableism – which won the Disability Film Festival. Sara is also the founder of Heretics Club: a literary salon for creative writers. She is currently pursuing her master's degree at Harvard University.

CAMILA RIVERA was born in Cali, Colombia and raised just about everywhere else. She is a witch, a wordsmith, and an eternal dreamer. Her work has been featured in online outlets such as *Frenshe* and *GoodGoodGood Co*.
All Things Friendship is Camila's first book and a dream come true. Ever the rolling stone, she splits her time between New Jersey and North Carolina. When she's not on the move, you can usually find her telling fortunes, singing bad karaoke, and working on her next novel.

MEET THE EXPERTS

Beth Lucas is a middle school counsellor for the Howard County Public School System in Fulton, Maryland, where she has worked for the last 25 years. Beth serves as a member of the Countywide Crisis Team and the Professional School Counsellors of Howard County, is a Student Assistance Programme Representative, and is one of her school's Rainbow Representatives. She earned a bachelor's degree in human development and family studies from Pennsylvania State University, a master's degree in school counseling from Loyola University Maryland, and a certificate in administration and supervision from Johns Hopkins University. Beth's favourite thing about working with adolescents is building relationships with her students and watching the tremendous growth they make from the time they enter sixth grade (year 7) to when they leave upon completing eighth grade (year 9). Outside of school, Beth enjoys crafting and travelling with her husband, Rich, and daughter, Mia.

Beth Lucas, School Counsellor

Alexandra Vaccaro, Psychotherapist

Alexandra Vaccaro is a licensed professional counsellor in the state of New Jersey. Alexandra earned her master's degree with high honours in counseling psychology from Felician University and completed her internship in out-patient therapy at Care Plus NJ, working with children, adolescents, and adults. Alexandra also obtained her 200-hour Registered Yoga Teacher (RYT) certification and Yoga Therapist certification. She incorporates yoga into therapy as an innovative approach for enhancing emotional health and wellness.

MORE FROM REBEL GIRLS

Let the stories of real-life women entertain and inspire you. Each volume in the Good Night Stories series includes 100 tales of extraordinary women.

Check out these mini books too!
Each one contains 25 stories about talented women, along with engaging activities.

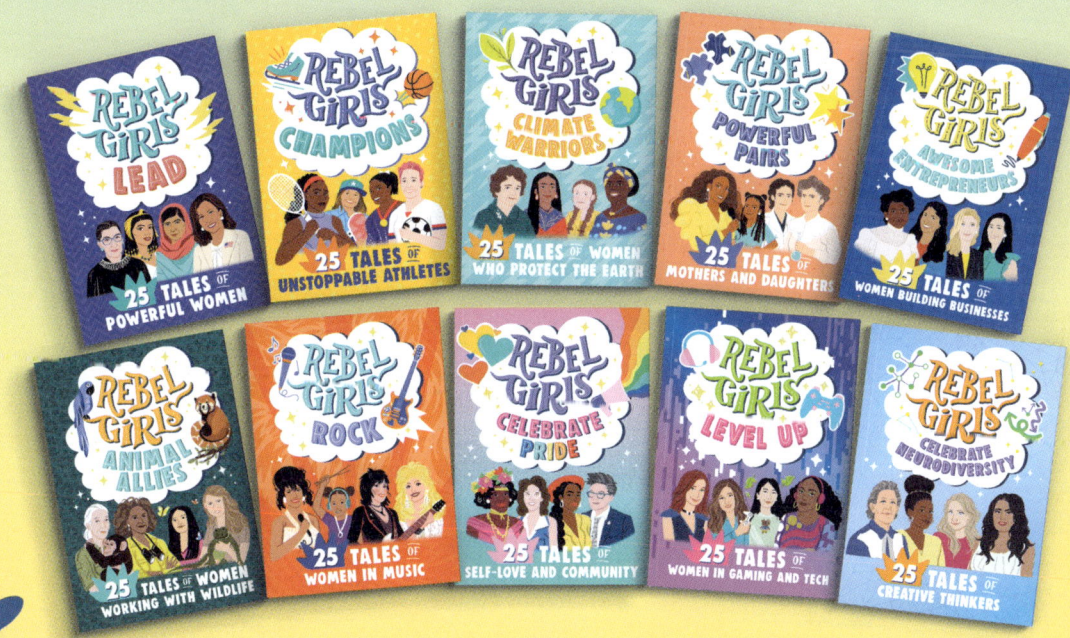

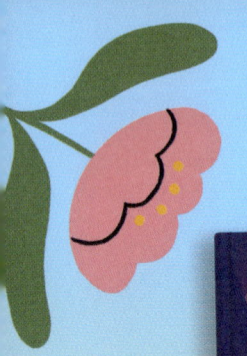

In *Dear Rebel*, more than 125 extraordinary teens and women share their advice, experiences, and the secrets of their success – in their own words.

Don't miss the rest of the bold, big-hearted guide-books in the Growing Up Powerful series.

156

The quirky questions in these books help curious readers explore their personalities, forecast their futures, and find common ground with extraordinary women who've come before them.

Dig deeper into the lives of these five real-life heroines with the Rebel Girls chapter book series.

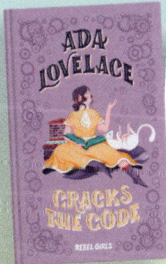

Uncover the groundbreaking inventions of Ada Lovelace, one of the world's first computer programmers.

Learn the exciting business of Madam C.J. Walker, the hair-care industry pioneer and first female self-made millionaire in the US.

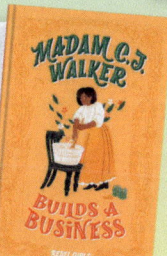

Explore the thrilling adventures of Junko Tabei, the first female climber to summit Mount Everest.

Discover the inspiring story of Dr. Wangari Maathai, the Nobel Peace Prize–winning environmental activist from Kenya.

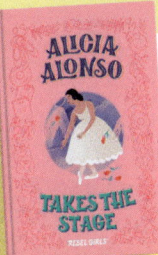

Follow the awe-inspiring career of Alicia Alonso, a world-renowned prima ballerina from Cuba.

REBEL GIRLS App

LISTEN TO MORE EMPOWERING STORIES ON THE REBEL GIRLS APP

Download the app to listen to beloved tales of extraordinary women. Filled with the adventures and accomplishments of women from around the world and throughout history, the Rebel Girls app is designed to entertain, inspire, and build confidence in listeners everywhere.

ABOUT REBEL GIRLS

REBEL GIRLS, a certified B Corporation, is a global, multi-platform empowerment brand dedicated to helping raise the most inspired and confident generation of girls through content, experiences, products, and community. Originating from an international best-selling children's book, Rebel Girls amplifies stories of real-life, extraordinary women throughout history, geography, and field of excellence. With a growing community of 30 million self-identified Rebel Girls spanning more than 100 countries, the brand engages with Generation Alpha through its book series, premier app and audio content, events, and merchandise. To date, Rebel Girls has sold more than 11 million books in 50 languages and reached 40 million audio listens. Award recognition includes the *New York Times* bestseller list, the 2022 Apple Design Award for Social Impact, multiple Webby Awards for family & kids and education, and Common Sense Media Selection honours, among others.

As a B Corp, we're part of a global community of businesses that meet high standards of social and environmental impact.

Join the Rebel Girls Community!

Visit rebelgirls.com and join our email list for exclusive sneak peeks, promos, activities, and more. You can also email us at hello@rebelgirls.com.

- YouTube: youtube.com/RebelGirls
- App: rebelgirls.com/audio
- Podcast: rebelgirls.com/podcast
- Facebook: facebook.com/rebelgirls
- Instagram: @rebelgirls
- Email: hello@rebelgirls.com
- Web: rebelgirls.com

If you liked this book, please take a moment to review it wherever you prefer!